Advance Praise for Champions in Life

Without knowing my goals or achievements I had no idea where I was going, or where I had been. It caused me to have a serious lack of identity. I felt like I was standing on the side of the road watching everyone else pass me by. The Brzyckis showed me that if you think life just happens to you, it actually ends up passing you by. You truly have to go out and make it your own.
—Teen

You really get to know yourself down deep inside . . . you grow and change.
It is a book about your life. This work is invaluable.
—Reader

I have used the Champions principles to change my entire family culture for the better!
—Parent

From the Back Cover

You are either building up your mental health every day, or letting the world tear it down.

People tend to talk about mental health only when something is wrong. This playbook is different. It builds proactive skills and protective factors so you can optimize your mental health and flourish—to the highest level of your hopes and dreams.

The only self-help book for teens that inspires you to experience who you are and want to become.

This playbook gives you a special place to really listen to your *own* thoughts and feelings. You will know that you belong and have a unique and important purpose in life. And you can express your amazing vision and commitment to other people to make the difference you want to make.

Learn 10 essential mental health skills to apply to your real life.

Each skill includes dynamic experiences for you to strengthen your self-esteem, self-confidence, resilience, and more. Feel all of your unique emotions and balance the many parts of your mind, body, and soul. Gain a genuine respect and love for who you are now and who you are becoming. Your ideas and emotions will shine like stars!

Champions in Life

Also by Elaine J. Brzycki and Henry G. Brzycki

Purpose and Possibilities: How to Transform Your Life
ISBN: 978-0-9887161-9-3

Mental Health for All Toolkit: Teachers, Parents, and Students
ISBN: 978-0-9887161-8-6

The Self in Schooling: How to Create Happy, Healthy, Flourishing People in the 21st Century
ISBN: 978-0-9887161-0-0

Student Success in Higher Education: Developing the Whole Person through High-Impact Practices
ISBN: 978-0-9887161-5-5

As Oito Etapas Para Alcançar o Bem-estar: Técnicas Simples e Eficazes Para Melhorar a Saúde Mental em um Mundo Acelerado (The Eight Steps to Achieving Well-Being: Simple and Effective Techniques to Improve Mental Health in a Fast-Paced World)
ISBN: 978- 65-5736-273-0

Champions in Life

The Playbook for Teens
and Their Parents with
10 Essential Skills to
Optimize Mental Health

Elaine J. Brzycki, Ed.M., and Henry G. Brzycki, Ph.D.

Champions in Life: The Playbook for Teens and Their Parents with 10 Essential Skills to Optimize Mental Health

Cover art and design by Paz Fernandez (PazArts.com)

Library of Congress Cataloging-in-Publication Data
Elaine J. Brzycki and Henry G. Brzycki, Champions in Life: The Playbook for Teens and Parents with 10 Essential Skills to Optimize Mental Health

Includes bibliographical references.
ISBN: 979-8-9921941-1-1 (IngramSpark);
               979-8-9921941-0-4 (Amazon paperback);
               979-8-9921941-2-8 (eBook)

1. Mental Health and Well-Being; 2. Psychological and Physical Well-Being; 3. Personal Growth and Development; 4. Teen Empowerment; 5. Self-Help for Teens

I. Title.
Library of Congress LCCN: 2025900274
Imprint Name: BG Publishing, State College, PA
Brzyckigroup.com

To each other

and

To all the teens in the world
for your extraordinary future

CONTENTS

Champions in Life

Introduction

Welcome to the *Champions in Life* playbook!

This playbook is dedicated to *you*, a teen in a truly monumental time in your life when many changes and new challenges arise.

You are amazing—just the way you are right now. No matter who you are, where you're from, or what you're going through—you are learning and growing. You deserve to be happy, healthy, and flourishing, now and always.

The *Champions in Life* playbook gives you skills and experiences to apply to your real life—so you can shine like a star!

You are either building up your mental health every day, or letting the world tear it down. "Mental health" means having a state of general well-being in your thoughts and emotions, so you can function and meet the ordinary demands of everyday life.

To "*optimize* mental health" goes beyond the basic definition of mental health. When you optimize your mental health, you are taking action to thrive in all areas of your life. You are going for the life of your dreams!

People tend to talk about mental health only when something is wrong. This playbook is different. It shows you that mental health is a wonderful part of being you. It builds proactive skills and protective factors to optimize your mental health, so you can really thrive and have a great life.

The playbook also helps you define what *you* mean by flourishing. What does having a great life look and feel like to *you*?

The playbook builds your resilience and other skills that optimize your mental health. Resilience is continuing to pursue a path, a project, or a task that is important to you, even when you hit a roadblock or obstacle that make it difficult to complete the project. Whatever the obstacles, you do it anyway!

What is a Playbook?

The *Champions in Life* playbook is the only self-help book for teens that helps you to discover *who you are* and *who you want to become.*

A "playbook" is a book, journal, or notebook that contains descriptions and examples of the kinds of skills and actions that can be taken to be successful in various situations in life. Examples are playbooks for putting on a theater production or winning a football game.

This playbook contains descriptions and examples of skills and actions you can take in your own day-to-day life to optimize your mental health. And better yet, by completing actual experiences, you will create the kinds of thoughts and actions that work best for you.

Note that the playbook uses the word "teen" to describe people in the general age range of 12 to 18 years. "Teen" is short for teenagers, adolescents, and young people experiencing puberty. You can actually be younger or older when reading this book, as some teen issues may begin earlier or extend into adulthood. Everybody grows up in their own way.

The playbook is all about the amazing parts of yourself that you don't always get the chance to notice and learn about.

You have other places to learn other things. For example, sports can be great for developing your physical body and teamwork. School can teach you academic skills such as adding and subtracting, and reading and writing. Music or art can free up your creativity. And reading stories or watching movies can give you a peek into other people's lives.

But this playbook is different than those other learning places. There are so many more parts of your mind that you need to experience, exercise, practice, and develop as you go through the rapid changes of your teen years.

The playbook gives you the chance to experience these amazing and important parts of you. These are the parts that will help you get through challenges, be happier, and go for your dreams.

The playbook provides approaches that you will actually *experience*. Then, you can apply them when you want in your life. When you really learn something, you always feel it inside and can do it again.

As an example, let's say you want to learn to ride a bicycle. You've got to get on the bicycle and feel the sense of balance, even though you may wobble, even fall a few times, or need someone to run alongside you. The skills and experiences in the playbook are similar to that.

When you learn about all of the many parts of your mind, body, and soul—*all* of the parts of yourself—and you find balance among all of these parts, then you are optimizing your mental health.

Just for You

The *Champions in Life* playbook is self-guided, so you can complete it at your own pace.

The playbook can also be challenging! You will feel and know that you really did something great when you complete it.

The *Champions in Life* playbook helps you to think and feel in ways that *you* want to think and feel, versus taking on what other people put on you. It builds skills that help you succeed in life to the highest level of your hopes and dreams, which provide you with your very own knowing about your unique potential and what is possible for you.

Above all, it is *your* playbook! It is your own *private* space, just for you! And then you can share your experiences with others—*if you want to!*

After completing the playbook, you will really know deep inside that you are a *Champion in Life*!

How to Involve Your Parent

It can be a source of growth, support, and encouragement to share your experiences with your parent or parents.

The playbook uses the word "parent" as shorthand to mean anyone who has the primary parenting responsibility for you.

That means you don't have to have a traditional family. Many different kinds of trusted, loving adults can serve the role of the "parent" in the playbook, such as parents, step-parents, guardians, foster parents, aunts, uncles, and grandparents.

The role of the "parent" could also be filled by *two* parents. Furthermore, it could even be filled by a counselor whom you and your parents have asked to be involved with the playbook.

Here are three ways you can use this playbook, with the third way being the one in which you involve your parent:

1. You can simply read about the 10 Essential Skills and learn new ideas. It is okay to do this, but the other two ways bring even more benefits.

2. An even better way to use this playbook is to not only read it, but also complete all of the experiences that go along with each skill. In this way, you can exercise each of the skills, actually see what works and doesn't work for you, learn them so they really stick with you, and realize you can apply them in many different situations. You can begin to optimize your mental health with every experience.

3. The playbook can have the biggest impact on your life if you not only read and experience it, but then also share—whatever you choose to share—with your parent. Since there are no right or wrong answers in the playbook, your parent's main role is to simply listen to you. It may feel unusual at first just to

be together in this way, but you will both get the hang of it. If you want, your parent can also serve as a guide to answer your questions about your experiences and talk to you about whatever you want to talk about.

The skills in this playbook are universal, meaning that they apply to *all* human beings. You and your parents can have any race, religion, nationality, gender, or abilities.

As you practice thinking and feeling for yourself, find ways to maintain your relationship with your parents. As adults, they have the benefit of life experience. At the same time, as a teen, you have a vital energy that cannot be denied. You both have something to give to each other.

Your parents love you, that is for certain. They have their own personalities, so they may show their love in ways that are different from other families. Whatever your parents are like, that is absolutely fine. Above all, they want you to have a great life.

How to Meet with Your Parent

When you meet with your parent, it will be a time to share *whatever you want* about your experiences with the playbook. Remember, your parents want you to develop your *own* ways of thinking and feeling, so you can practice optimizing your mental and physical health, and know who you are and want to become.

How often should you meet with your parent? That depends on how much time you want to take with each skill and how much you want to involve them. It is up to you.

One example would be to do one of the 10 Essential Skills per week. In this case, set up a time each week when you meet with your parent to talk about the skill and what you experienced, or to share whatever you would like.

But you can actually be very flexible and take *as long as you need* for each skill. For example, if you take months to complete the skills, they may unfold more naturally and less on a specific timetable. If you take this longer approach, simply meet with your parent every so often to check in with each other.

If you have brothers and sisters, they can each have their own time with your parent. This time is just for *you* and your parent.

This is very different from most things in your life. When you meet, *you* actually let your parents know what is going on and what you're trying to do. It is not the other way around, like it is most of the time.

Share This with Your Parent

It can help to let your parent know what your meetings will be about. If you don't have the exact words to say to your parent, simply ask your parent to read the description on the following page, or you can read it to them out loud. If it feels odd using words you didn't write, you will have plenty of opportunity throughout the playbook to use your own words.

But for now, when you want to get started with the playbook, please feel free to use the description or build off of it.

Here is what to have your parent read or you read to them:

"I'm working on building up my mental health skills so I can have the life of my dreams. I want to be proactive and develop preventative skills so I can optimize my mental health. I want to be more resilient and prepared for whatever comes my way—the ups and downs, and everything in between. The *Champions in Life* playbook is all about me at a really important time in my life when so much is changing in my body and mind.

In the self-guided playbook, there are no right or wrong answers. There are 10 Essential Skills in the playbook, and I would like to meet with you after I complete each one. In this way, I can show you who I am becoming, and you can support me in developing my optimal mental health. I don't need you to be perfect or have any answers for me.

Your role during our meetings is to mostly just listen, so I can have my own experiences and tell you about them in the way that works best for me. After I have a chance to share what's going on with me, if you have something you want to share from your own experiences, that's good too.

We're always so busy, or online, or working, and there is a time and place for all that. But this is different. Sometimes we might just sit and not talk much or just look at a picture I drew. I need for you to believe in me and give me the space to practice forming my own identity and making my own choices, because that is how I will thrive the most in my own life. I know you love me. I really appreciate it when you show that you love me just for being me, and not just when I get good grades. I love you. Thanks!"

How to Complete the 10 Essential Skills

The *Champions in Life* playbook has 10 different sections. Each section describes one of the "10 Essential Skills to Optimize Mental Health."

The 10 Essential Skills are:
- Create Context
- Experience Emotions
- Know Your Inner and Outer Self
- Connect Mind and Body
- Dream Big Dreams
- Discover Your Unique Purpose
- Commit
- Communicate
- Contribute
- Celebrate You

Each of the skills are important, because they:

- help you build a truly happy, healthy, and extraordinary life;

- apply to all human beings, so no matter where you are in your life, you can experience and develop them;

- help you get more of what you want, so you can flourish and experience your life more fully, with more happiness and vitality;

- help you experience new possibilities in the way you see yourself and the world;

- show that you can have an impact on other people, just by being who you are; and

- provide preventative skills and protective factors *before* you need them, so you have resilience and are ready for life's ups and downs.

As you complete the playbook, you will be learning to access new experiences of who you are and want to become. You will gain a deeper awareness of what it means to have a "self," with feelings and thoughts that are unique to you.

Each of the skills in this book can develop over time, getting stronger and stronger. For example, imagine a little child learning to throw a ball. In throwing the ball, the little child is trying out a new skill, so the ball won't travel too far. But then, as the child grows up, they might get really interested in throwing balls, practice a lot, and even learn to pitch a baseball or a softball.

Now you wouldn't expect someone just learning to throw a ball for the very first time to be able to immediately pitch a speedy baseball or softball, would you? In the same way, you can experience the skills in this playbook, as if you were trying them out for the very first time.

Once you have completed all of the sections in this playbook, you will have developed many new abilities that you really value. And you will really know that you are a *Champion in Life*! Hurray!

How to Complete the Experiences

Each of the 10 Essential Skills has three "experiences" that go along with the skill. These "experiences" are activities that you actually do or create in your real life.

A little star (that looks like this: ★) marks the spot where the playbook tells you the specific actions you will take to complete the experience.

Complete the experiences in order to practice the skill and demonstrate it in your own life. Finally, share the parts of your experiences that you want to share with your parent.

To complete an experience, think about what the experience is asking you to do. Be aware of what you are feeling, thinking, and doing to complete the experience. Next, you will do something to represent that you participated and completed the experience. The experiences generally come in three types:

- Some experiences are actions—such as saying words out loud, or doing something in your life that you have never done before.

- Other experiences ask you to describe what you discover, realize, or dream up.

- And other experiences ask you to use your creativity to make or create something, such as a drawing, video, music, and more.

One approach is to write and draw about your experiences directly into this playbook. You can write poems or prose. Feel free to write, doodle, draw, highlight, or sketch anywhere in the playbook, on any page. Remember, it is *your* playbook! And it is your own *private* space, just for you! You can share your experiences with others *only if you want to!*

Your drawings and sketches do *not* need to be realistic at all—no art skills required! A bright yellow blob can mean "happiness," or a blue squiggle can mean "peaceful." Just go with the main idea you want to express.

You may want to use more space, for example, by drawing or writing on bigger pieces of paper, or in a notebook that you or your parent purchase. When you use your hands in physical ways, such as drawing or writing by hand, it helps to form special connections between your hands and brain that really make the experience last.

Then again, you may prefer to write, draw, or make a video directly on a computer. That is fine, if that is what you choose to do. If you happen to be reading this on an e-book reader, you will either need to be able to write and draw on your screen, or alternatively, use a separate notebook.

You have the freedom to complete the experiences in lots of different ways, depending upon what works best for you.

You can make a movie or documentary of your experiences, write music that describes your emotions, create a new dance that expresses your feelings, or use a combination of all these methods of self-expression. It will be very exciting to see what you create!

You may even think of other ways to represent the experiences that go beyond the space of the playbook, for instance, run, bake, swim, hike, play sports . . . you name it! Just be sure to make some kind of record for yourself of your thoughts, feelings, and responses to the experiences.

When you engage in the experiences, feel free to bring in all of the challenges in all areas of your life. You can use the experiences to get stronger in your friendships, your family relationships, your own abilities to feel, and your growth as a person. In learning new skills, you may also notice that you have new or previously hidden talents and strengths.

When completing each experience, notice if an experience feels easy, hard, fun, silly, uplifting, or any other qualities, both good and bad. Whatever you are feeling about the experience is fine.

When it all comes down to it, the vital action is to simply complete the experiences. Most importantly, these experiences are all about you and what *you* want—they are *not* about what *other* people want.

As you already know, there are plenty of other places in your life where it may be appropriate to respond to what other people want. But this playbook is about you! You do *not* have to be perfect! You don't have to agree with everything. You actually don't even have to understand every word or concept in the playbook.

To optimize your mental health, you *do* have to try your best to complete the experiences in order to practice and develop the skills. At the end of the playbook, you can choose the experiences and skills that worked best for you and that you can see yourself using again in your life. *You* get to choose which experiences are the most important to you. You can decide which experiences—just like the "plays" to use in a sporting event—are ones you want to use again to make your life great day-to-day.

You may see changes in how you think and feel as you complete the experiences. All people, you included, are constantly changing anyway, so you may as well take charge of the process of change and go in the direction you want. It is in your self-interest to change—you benefit!

How Did You Do?

Throughout the playbook, when you get to the end of each of the 10 Essential Skills, you will have the opportunity to assess how you think you did on that skill. This is *not* a test like you get in school. Assessing *for yourself* how you did is an important step. As a *Champion in Life*, you want to be challenged, and optimal mental health develops when you learn about your "inner self."

For example, when you hear someone who is really good at a sport talk about their skills, they measure themselves by their *own* benchmarks. It is an amazing practice.

If they are too hard on themselves and too perfectionistic, then they don't allow any room to try new things or even enjoy their sport. But if they set their benchmark too low and too easy, then they lose the opportunity to challenge themselves, grow, and continually get better.

When a sports champion measures their performance by their own benchmarks, then all the judgements of the outside world don't matter all that much. It is all about their own choices and values.

Like the sports champion, it is up to you to determine for yourself what your highest level looks and feels like. At first, you may be too hard on yourself, or too easy. But soon you will find the right balance! You will actually get better at assessing yourself as you move through the playbook. Try it!

After you complete all of the experiences for each skill, the playbook will prompt you to assess yourself on how you did overall on the skill.

The playbook will ask you these questions:

- Did you complete all of the experiences for this skill?
- Describe which experience was the most meaningful to you.
- In the space below, draw 1 to 5 stars. Give yourself at least 1 star for completing all the experiences and up to 5 stars if you feel you did great on this skill overall.

Here is an example of one way to respond to the questions:

- Yes, the experiences are all complete. I wrote my thoughts in the playbook, and I drew a picture of my feelings.
- It was meaningful, because I tried out the experiences in my life and felt really proud of myself for taking the chance.
- I give myself 5 stars, because I really worked hard on being real with myself about what I was feeling, not what I thought someone else wanted me to feel.

After you have read about the skill, completed each of the experiences for the skill, and done your self-assessment, then it is time to share your thoughts and feelings with your parent.

Certificates of Accomplishment

Finally, at the end of each of the 10 Essential Skills, after you complete all of the experiences for that skill, you will be able to award yourself a *Certificate of Accomplishment* for the skill you learned. By the end of the playbook, you will have 10 *Certificates of Accomplishment*.

And there is one more! After the 10 *Certificates of Accomplishment*, you will be able to award yourself the *final* certificate that declares you have earned the title of a true *Champion in Life*!

Feel free to color, decorate, and write your name on the *Certificates* in any way that you like.

To earn all of the *Certificates*, honor yourself, do what you say you are going to do, and complete the experiences.

Champions in Life on Instagram

The *Champions in Life* playbook encourages you to freely choose to spend time *away* from the screen to do activities that makes you feel *human*, such as walking in the rain, singing silly songs, doing crafts, playing something fun, or hugging someone.

But you may get a lot out of participating on social media. So, if it is helpful and you want to connect with other teens who are becoming *Champions in Life*, the playbook has set up an Instagram account.

If you want, share pictures, writing, or other records of your *Champions in Life* experiences. Encourage other *Champions in Life* to keep going!

And be sure to ask your parent if it is okay with them if you post.

And you totally do *not* have to share anything. Maybe you are not on social media, which is absolutely fine. Or maybe you want this playbook to be the one thing in your life that actually stays *off* of social media.

The Instagram account is meant for teens to talk to other teens about optimizing mental health and becoming *Champions in Life*. On occasion, the authors of the playbook will post encouragement or sections of the playbook.

The Instagram account is a place where everyone uplifts and encourages each other to be *Champions in Life*. But you can be real. You don't have to be happy and confident all the time.

If you get the urge to compare yourself to someone else, simply stop and ask yourself what aspects of that person's experience you admire and may want to experience yourself. Then share your *own* challenges, hopes, and dreams. Your thoughts and emotions are perfectly fine just the way they are!

In sum, posting is totally *optional.* The Instagram account is offered for those who like it. If you find sharing on social media to be fun and encouraging, go for it!

Here is the Instagram account:
champions_in_life_teen

You can also share your experiences with the authors of the playbook at:
brzyckigroup.com

Though the authors may not be able to respond to every teen who reaches out, they will happily celebrate all of your good work on yourself!

Optimize Your Mental Health and Flourish

As you complete the playbook, always come back to the intention to optimize your mental health. To "optimize" mental health is an action, while "optimal" mental health means a state of being. Both "optimize" and "optimal" are used throughout the playbook.

Having optimal mental health means you:

- have strong protective factors that support you no matter what life throws your way, through all of life's ups and downs;

- are taking action to have well-being in all areas of your life.

Most of all, when you optimize your mental health, you can truly flourish in your life. "Flourish" means to go after your highest dreams for your life—the kind of dreams you have when you are awake and strongly desire something beautiful and wonderful. You are going for much more than "just getting by" or just surviving. You can have a great life!

When you flourish, your emotions are soaring. You dream of a life that is so extraordinary that it blows you away and the other people you talk to about it. Your experience is so different and filled with amazing new ideas. Flourishing feels like when you have so much energy, that the top of your head will come off and brilliant stars will explode upwards!

You have the *courage* to dream of a life that exceeds your previously conceived expectations. You truly love yourself just as you are now and who you hope to become. You share your heartfelt feelings with people you love and care about. You have a deep commitment to contribute to other people.

Your life is filled with many experiences that are very meaningful to you, and you are constantly in touch with that meaning. You are taking action to have the life of your dreams!

A Simple Tool to Get You Started

Before moving on to learning the 10 Essential Skills in the playbook, take a moment to consider the current state of your mental health by your own definition. The Optimal Mental Health Scale is not a grade, nor a test of intelligence, nor a final judgement of your worth. It is simply a tool.

Mental health can be considered on a scale. If you are at "0," then you are getting by in life. Negative numbers indicate that you feel you are struggling. The positive numbers indicate you are often experiencing a sense of flourishing. Circle the number you feel you are at now.

Champions in Life
Optimal Mental Health Scale

| -5 | -4 | -3 | -2 | -1 | 0 | +1 | +2 | +3 | +4 | +5 |

⬅ Low mental health   Optimal mental health and flourishing ➡

Simply by observing yourself in this way, you are developing optimal mental health. You are becoming a *Champion in Life*!

Learn the

10 Essential Skills

to

Optimize Mental Health

Skill 1

Create Context

Be aware of what setting or mood you are in, and then actually begin to create, initiate, or change a setting or mood.

Create Context

The first essential skill for optimal mental health is called "create context." This skill is so important, because when you do it, you literally create who you are and your reality of life. Wow, a pretty powerful idea, right?

Before you can "create context," it is helpful to know what "context" is.

"Context" is a setting, mood, or environment in which something takes place.

To "be aware of context" means that you have knowledge—of a setting, mood, or environment in which something takes place—gained through your own senses and mind. You are aware of your thoughts and feelings, bodily sensations, physical surroundings, and your intentions to experience the setting or mood.

To "create context" means you can actually begin to change, initiate, invent, or create the setting or mood that you are in. You make it happen!

These are examples of different kinds of context. As you read the examples, try to imagine times when you were in that context and how you felt. If you think of other examples, jot them down in the open spaces below.

Mood
- Time
- Thoughts
- Attitudes
- Emotions
- Feelings

Place
- Home
- Relative's home
- School

- Park
- Place of religious worship

Nature

- Thunderstorm
- Heat
- Sun
- Cold
- Forest

Events

- Birthday party
- Graduation
- Game
- Listening to music

People

- Family
- Friends
- Classmates
- Teachers
- Self

Technology and Media

- Social media
- Games
- Artificial intelligence
- Online information
- News

Other Examples of Context

-
-

Sometimes context is shaped by your natural surroundings. You wear a jacket as a response to cold weather. Pretty simple, right?

Other times, context is primarily determined, shaped, or created by *other people*. You can begin by being aware of whether a context is in real life (such as a family dinner) or in a made-up world (such as a video game). You can also choose which contexts are more important to you and which ones are less important.

Further, you can decide how you will respond to a particular context. Maybe you feel it is best to simply observe a context to better understand it. That is absolutely fine. Then again, maybe you feel it is best to participate fully in the context. For instance, if everyone is dancing to your favorite music, you can decide to join in the fun and let go!

Finally, context can be determined, shaped, or created by *you*. You can make it happen! When you create context, you are clear how you want to participate in life's moments for your own well-being. You can really experience your feelings, emotions, and thoughts as you create the context.

When you can create context, you are promoting a part of yourself called "internal motivation," which means you decide for yourself what you want to go after and get.

You are also developing a part of yourself called "self-efficacy," which means that more often than not, you make things happen, rather than everything just happening to you. Further, you are developing a belief that you can accomplish what you set out to accomplish.

Finally, you are learning that you are in control of your own destiny in life, a trait called "self-determination." This means that you are taking responsibility for the future "self" that you want to create.

Now it is time to take on the experiences that go along with this skill and see how they fit in your real life.

Create Context

Experience 1
Flourishing

In this experience, you will choose a context that is important to you and then show yourself being really great in that context. Context can be an attitude, person, place, activity, environment, event, or something else that you want to experience.

Being really great can include all sorts of emotions. Consider what emotions you want to feel. It can help to answer the question: "What does it look and feel like to be great in this context?"

Go for "flourishing" when you choose your context. As your learned earlier in this section, "flourishing" means to go after your highest dreams, pursue more than the ordinary, and move in the direction of new possibilities. Flourishing is also your *own* definition of what is really great for you.

For example, you might choose "friendships" as your context. Think about what it feels like for you to experience being and having a truly great friend.

Now it is time to experience flourishing! Choose a context that is important to you. Create something—through writing, drawing, or some other activity—that represents that you are really flourishing in the context you just chose. You can be flourishing now, or have a vision to flourish in the future. As discussed earlier, you can use words, drawings, photos, videos, music, sports, dance, or many other approaches to represent this experience.

There are no "right" or "wrong" answers! Make it up! Choose one context and create something that represents you being great and flourishing in that context. Just get started! Go for it!

I choose this context:

This is how it feels to flourish and be really great in this context:

Create Context

Experience 2
Affirmations

It may be strange to think of your own mind as a context, but it actually is.

Your "mind" is that part of you that feels, perceives, thinks, imagines, desires, and remembers.

Your own mind is a context that you take with you, wherever you go. You can create your own context.

Now you will experience "affirmations," which are when you declare something positive and encouraging to yourself. Affirmations demonstrate something called "positive self-talk." You are actually learning how to rewire your brain from negative to positive views of your life. You are creating the space for new thoughts and feelings about yourself and your future.

When doing this experience, if you hear your mind thinking any negative judgements about yourself, simply say, "Hey, thanks for sharing your opinion, but save it for later! I'm doing something else now!" And then keep going with the experience!

There are two ways to do this experience. Choose one or both of the following activities:

1. Look in the mirror at yourself, directly into your eyes. Take a moment to get over how weird this feels! You can do it! Look only in your eyes, as if you are communicating with the person in the mirror. Then say these phrases to yourself either out loud or mouthing the words silently, while still looking directly into your own eyes:

"I am doing my best!"
"I can do this!"
"I am a *Champion in Life*!"

2. Or, you can do this without the mirror. Close your eyes and put your hand on your heart. Feel it beating. With your hand still on your heart, say these phrases:

"I am doing my best!"
"I can do this!"
"I am a *Champion in Life*!"

Do one or both of these activities every day for 4 days.

This is something you do; you don't just sit and think about it.

What did it feel like to say the affirmations?

Create Context

Experience 3
Possibilities

This experience helps show you what a new possibility feels like. You will create a context with a new possibility, by impacting or changing what is going on in a particular situation.

For example, you walk into the lunch room at school and notice that your friends with whom you usually sit are not at your usual table.

The lunch room is a context. So, you now see that this context is different than most days. It throws you off at first. But then, you decide to create your own context though a new possibility. Here's how you do it:

You choose to sit with others who you know and would like to know better.

When you do this, you are taking a risk to interact with other people, meaning that you are doing something that you have never done before, which can be scary and filled with fear. Don't let that stop you. Feel the fear and do the action anyway—you can do it! That is how you create context with a new possibility.

For this experience, choose a context in your real life. You can choose the exact same situation as in the example, or choose another similar situation. As you go through the day, notice the context. Ask yourself, "Do I want to impact this context with a new possibility?" If yes, "What do I want to do?" Then choose to impact or change what is going on in that particular situation.

Now, try it out!

How did it go? Did it go great? Hurray!

Did it come out differently than you thought? That's all good too—you took the risk to interact with other people, and you are a brave and awesome human being!

Create Context

How Did You Do?

Assess yourself on how you did on this skill. Ask yourself these questions:
- Did you complete all of the experiences for this skill?
- Describe which experience was the most meaningful to you.
- In the space below, draw 1 to 5 stars. Give yourself at least 1 star for completing all the experiences and up to 5 stars if you feel you did great on this skill overall.

Meet with Your Parent

Take a look back at everything you did for this skill and choose something to share with your parent. You can choose to share something you:
- learned about yourself
- are feeling
- created or made
- are doing to flourish and build your optimal mental health
- want to ask your parent about
- want to ask your parent to help you do
- and more

It is up to you to choose what you want to share about this skill. Remember, this is one meeting in your life when it is all about *you*, so you can practice having optimal mental health. There are no right or wrong answers! Your meeting doesn't have to be perfect. Give it a try!

Champions in Life

CERTIFICATE OF ACCOMPLISHMENT

Optimal Mental Health Superstar Award
for Completing Skill 1

Create Context

_____
completed all of the experiences of the Create Context skill.

Let Your Star Shine!

Skill 2

Experience Emotions

*Fully experience your unique emotions and
realize that your feelings can be different from what other people feel.*

Experience Emotions

Fully experiencing your feelings and emotions is an important skill to optimize your mental health. To experience your emotions means to feel and be present to what is going on inside of you in any given situation.

You are the only one of your kind! Because you are "unique," by definition you are without equal, extraordinary, and special. You have unique skills and talents that will change and grow throughout your life.

Even more importantly, you have unique *emotions* that no one else has. You have unique ways of sensing, thinking, and feeling which make everything you do a special contribution.

"Emotions" and "feelings" are often used interchangeably, though you can keep a slight difference in mind. When you experience your unique "emotions," you have sensations that tell you something is happening. Then, you experience "feelings" by assigning a description or meaning to the sensations. Finally, you can decide when to share what you feel. You can do it!

Read these examples of how your emotions and feelings are unique. As you read these examples, think of times when you might have experienced them. Recall whether it seemed like your feelings were *similar* to what everyone else around you seemed to be experiencing, or if what you were feeling was completely *different*. Either way is great!

- Thoughtful
- Playful
- Confident
- Lazy
- Happy
- Confused
- Curious
- Reflective

- Alert
- Thrilled
- Excited
- Regretful
- Frustrated
- Jealous
- Angry
- Bold
- Cautious
- Amazed
- Sad
- Loving
- Wishful
- Inspired
- In awe
- . . . and more
- . . . What other emotions can you think of?

There are hundreds of different ways to experience your unique emotions and feelings. You can even combine feelings, such as "happy *and* sad" and "in awe *and* inspired."

How you decide to experience your unique emotions is up to you. You may feel happy for no reason and just want to keep a quiet smile to yourself. You may be feeling very caring and choose to share your caring emotions by helping your parents or friends with something they are doing.

You can share your choices, promises, self-reliance, personal best, hopes and dreams, and so on. Whenever you share something that is real for you, you are making a unique contribution.

Everyone Has Difficult Emotions Sometimes

Sometimes the people who love you attempt to protect you from sad or hard moments. Then, when those sad or hard moments come up, or when everything doesn't go perfectly, you might actually think something is wrong with you. Just remember, you are fine the way you are! You are fully capable of handling the sad and hard moments in your own way!

Experiencing strong emotions *does* take lots of practice. You have to work on it every day. The playbook has some suggestions for you to consider, so you can continue to build your optimal mental health.

You can optimize your mental health when you imagine your emotions as a river flowing through you. Many different emotions will come and go—every day.

To fully experience your emotions:
- Really feel the emotion first, and let it flow through you.
- Notice what sensations are happening in your body when you feel the emotion.
- Identify the emotion, and give it a name.
- Say to yourself what you really want next.
- Choose whether or not to take some kind of action.

For example, when feeling anxious, this is a good time to practice being in your body. Identify everything going on with your body. Is your stomach in knots? Are you breathing fast? Do you feel like running away? Then take five big breaths. And five big breaths again. Now ask yourself, "What do I really want next?" Often, you will realize you can do it, and you will decide to keep going, even if you are anxious about what will happen.

When you are sad, feel free to cry and get it all out. Feeling sad is perfectly normal and good, because it tells you that you are disappointed, or you did not get the outcome or result that you wanted. Crying is a normal and healthy release for people of all genders. Sadness is best felt and then released. Don't plug it up. It is okay to listen to sad music or draw a sad picture. Then, identify what you are

39

sad about. Be as specific as you can. After you feel it, say to yourself what you really want next. Finally, come up with a plan to move on. What's next?

Sometimes sadness is grief for something that you have lost. Maybe a friend has moved away, as an example. Or sometimes an entire family is grieving a loss. When sadness is grief, it may take longer to experience. Talking to your parents about it can help. It is totally normal to grieve losses. Take care of your grief as if it were a little child inside of you. Be gentle and patient with this little child. One day the little child will be strong enough to play again!

When you first feel anger or frustration, you might want to lash out. Or you might want to shove it down and pretend you are not angry. But it is better when you are angry or frustrated to step back for a while and take a good long moment to figure out what you're so angry about. Take a lot of time! Ask yourself, did someone say something, and then you felt embarrassed? Or did it feel like you were stopped from doing what you wanted? Did you make what you thought was a mistake that you wish no one else had seen? Identify who or what you are mad at.

Then it is important to say to yourself what you *want* next. Once you are a bit clearer about what made you so angry and what you want next, try out different approaches in your mind. Now that you have a better idea of what you're feeling and what you want, you can talk to your parent about what you can do next to move past your anger, move in the direction of what you want, and get back to other experiences and feelings.

If a difficult emotion does get to be too much at some point, or it seems to be lasting forever, be up front and request help from your parent when you need it, and then decide next steps together.

Experiencing your difficult emotions takes practice!

Feel the Good Emotions Too!

What about happy feelings? It can take just as much practice to consider all the wonderful emotions and feelings that you want to enjoy, cherish, take delight in, value, and appreciate.

Take a moment to *notice* and *savor* when you:

- giggle, feel happy, or are joyful, even for no reason at all
- laugh until your stomach hurts
- feel a sense of awe, like when you see a rainbow glow above the clouds, or your favorite sports figure does an incredible move on the field or court
- feel affection and love for other people—your parents, other family members, and friends
- have genuine love for yourself—you're amazing!

Emotions and feelings are fascinating! Experience all of them! You're on your way to being a *Champion in Life*!

Experience Emotions

Experience 1
Create a Feeling

You can *want* whatever you *want*. It is up to you!

Sometimes it is easier to want things that you can physically touch. For example, you may want an ice cream cone. You can touch, taste, smell, see, and even hear the cone crunch. Your experience tells you it tastes good, it's melting so you have to eat it fast, and you're laughing as it drips.

For this experience, you will describe something that you *want to feel on the inside*. It can include feelings, moods, or attitudes.

For example, "I want to feel like I am great just the way I am now, and I like myself."

Then you will name three other feelings that go along with the primary feeling you want.

For example, "When I feel like I am great just the way I am now, and I like myself, then:
1) I feel more loved by family and friends."
2) I feel more relaxed around other people."
3) negative people don't bother me as much."

If you don't know what you want to feel, then for this exercise, simply make something up. Choose any positive emotion as a practice run. Then continue with the exercise.

You are learning in this experience that you can create your own feelings and emotions, even happiness. You are also learning what is called "emotional intelligence," which is when you experience emotions and then regulate or determine what to do with these emotions. You are more aware of your emotions, so you can make decisions about them, instead of your emotions controlling you.

Right now, at this very moment, write down or draw what you want to feel inside.

"I want to feel . . ."

Now describe three more feeling, moods, or attitudes that go along with the primary feeling you want. Take a look at the previous example, if that helps you get started.

1.

2.

3.

Space for Writing and Drawing

Experience Emotions

Experience 2
Self-Affect

"Self-affect" is the ability to "really experience your emotions and feelings."

It is the exact opposite of feeling numb.

You may say, "That's obvious! Of course, I experience my feelings!" But not so fast! Sometimes the teen years can bring so much change, that a teen might numb their feelings, and actually not experience them anymore. They may attempt to shove down their feelings.

To have optimal mental health, you need "be present" to your full life, along with your strong emotions and feelings. To "be present" means to be aware, in touch with, or real with yourself about each moment.

Choose a time or an event when you felt a powerful emotion or feeling. It can be any feeling. Now describe, draw, or demonstrate the following information about the feeling you chose. Remember, you can always draw on other pieces of paper if you need more room. Or make a video, do a dance, or anything to describe the time when you experienced this powerful feeling.

- What was the feeling or emotion?
- Where did the feeling take place?
- When was it?
- Who was there?
- What happened?
- How long did you feel that way?

There are no right or wrong answers!

Space for Writing and Drawing

Experience Emotions

Experience 3
Share a Feeling

Fully experiencing your feelings often includes sharing them with other people. When you share a happy feeling with another person, many times your happiness will grow. When you share a sad feeling, it might feel less heavy.

Most of all, sharing a feeling connects you with other people, which is a great experience in life. Sharing a feeling takes courage, because you never know how the other person will feel or react. *Champions in Life* continue to learn how to share their feelings at the right time and place. It takes practice!

In this exercise, you will be telling someone out loud that you have a feeling. Tell them respectfully and truthfully. Choose from excited, happy, frustrated, sad, excited, in awe, or any other feeling you can imagine. Tell someone in person, rather than by text or social media, although a video chat or phone call could be an acceptable option. Tell someone you know, like, and trust, such as your parent, a friend, a teacher, a coach, or another family member. You can write down what you want to say before you say it.

Sometimes, when you tell a person your feeling, it leads to more conversation. While other times, sharing a feeling can result in a big hug. Be prepared to listen to how the other person responds. They may say they share similar feelings, such as when you are both excited about something fun.

Some feelings take longer to share. If the feeling you share is sad or anxious, the other person may try to cheer you up or help you overcome your fears. If you are angry and that is the feeling you decide to share, they may want to be helpful and give advice about what to do next. Be prepared to listen if they start talking. Notice how you are feeling when the other person speaks.

And if you don't want any advice, help, or cheering up, simply tell the person. The most important aspect of this exercise is to share a feeling.

★

This is a challenging experience, but you can do it!

Now it is time to choose your feeling and share it out loud with someone. Here is one approach to use, or come up with something entirely your own:

"I want to share something with you. I just want you to know. Right now, I feel:"

"I wanted to share this feeling with you. Thank you for listening."

If you don't want advice, you can continue to say:

"You don't need to say anything or give any advice. I just wanted to share my feeling so I know it is real."

If you are open to receiving some advice, then be proactive and ask for advice or cheering up:

"I'm actually telling you so that you can give me some [cheering up, help, advice]. Got any?"

Better yet, ask them a time when they had a similar feeling, so they can share an actual experience.

Now listen to what the other person says.

Notice what you are feeling inside when it is their turn to speak.

Experience Emotions

How Did You Do?

Assess yourself on how you did on this skill. Ask yourself these questions:

- Did you complete all of the experiences for this skill?
- Describe which experience was the most meaningful to you.
- In the space below, draw 1 to 5 stars. Give yourself at least 1 star for completing all the experiences and up to 5 stars if you feel you did great on this skill overall.

Meet with Your Parent

Take a look back at everything you did for this skill and choose something to share with your parent. You can choose to share something you:

- learned about yourself
- are feeling
- created or made
- are doing to flourish and build your optimal mental health
- want to ask your parent about
- want to ask your parent to help you do
- and more

It is up to you to choose what you want to share about this skill. Remember, this is one meeting in your life when it is all about *you*, so you can practice having optimal mental health. There are no right or wrong answers! Your meeting doesn't have to be perfect. Give it a try!

Champions in Life

CERTIFICATE OF ACCOMPLISHMENT

Optimal Mental Health Superstar Award
for Completing Skill 2

Experience Emotions

_____

completed all of the experiences of the Experience Emotions skill.

Let Your Star Shine!

Skill 3

Know Your Inner and Outer Self

*Your "inner self" thinks and feels what you want,
and then your "outer self" chooses the best time and place to
express your thoughts and feelings to other people.*

Know Your Inner and Outer Self

You can have feelings and thoughts on the *inside* of yourself, and then make choices what to do to bring your feelings and thoughts *outside* yourself. Your "inner self" decides when to connect with your "outer self."

In short, you are in charge. You have your hands on the steering wheel of your life. You decide what do with your inner feelings and thoughts.

You Have an Amazing "Self"

Before learning about your "inner self" and your "outer self," you need to be aware of what a "self" is. Your "self" consists of all the elements that make you an individual person—your body, mind, emotions, thoughts, desires, and sensations.

Up until now in your life, you didn't need to give much thought to having a "self." As a child, it was good that adults protected you by guiding your every move.

But now, as a teen, you are suddenly bombarded with lots of contexts trying to tell you what to feel and think:

- Your school tests and grades you so much that you begin to feel like a piece of data instead of a human being.
- Everyone seems to want you to be good at every single thing you do.
- Your peers all seem to be so much more in control (actually, they are not, but it often feels that way).
- Then, when classmates say mean things like they sometimes do (stemming from their own teen issues), it seems to really hurt and land a punch like it never did before.
- On top of all that, social media constantly tells you what to do, think, or buy in order to fit in.
- And suddenly, your family doesn't seem to understand everything you are going through. Ugh!

The answer to this bombardment is to become more and more "self-aware."

To be "self-aware" means you are aware of your "self." It means you realize, perceive, and notice your *own* ways of sensing, thinking, and feeling. To be self-aware is to know all of your qualities. Being self-aware, you have more resilience. And remarkably, you have more strength to give to others in order to make the difference you want to make.

Being self-aware also happens to be the number one protective factor to achieve optimal mental health. So, learning about the "self" is a big deal!

Furthermore, the "self" consists of 40 "attributes" that make up what is known as the Integrated Self Model™. "Attributes" are the qualities and characteristics of an individual.

Many of these attributes are mentioned throughout the playbook as part of the skills and experiences. Simply *experience* the attributes throughout the playbook. However, if you are interested in reading more about them, the full Integrated Self Model™ is described in the last section of this playbook.

Throughout your life, you want to learn how to *integrate* (bring together) all of your different attributes to create a whole "self." Life today has many forces that attempt to *disintegrate* (tear apart) your "self." Your challenge as a *Champion in Life* is to use your unique attributes to not let that happen.

No matter who you are, or where you are from, you have a beautiful "inner self." As an expert in integrative medicine writes:

The core self contains an essential humanity whose nature is peace and whose expression is thought and whose action is unconditional love.
When we identify with that inner core, respecting and honoring it in others as well as ourselves, we experience healing in every area of our lives.
—Joan Borysenko

Your Inner Self . . .

- is very powerful and exciting
- has the courage to come up with your own ideas
- listens to the "I Can Do It!" voice
- experiences sensations
- has feelings and emotions
- has thoughts that are uniquely your own
- is private—only you can know what you are feeling and thinking
- explores what is possible
- creates "what if" scenarios

No one else can see or hear inside your "inner self." Therefore, you have to bring it out by using your "outer self" so that you can have great relationships and make your life happen.

Your Outer Self . . .

- takes the risk to be heard
- takes the risk to impact other people
- can ignore negative people, or can deal with them too
- can choose to express your inner feelings and emotions, or choose *not* to express them

Examples of Inner and Outer Self

Your "inner self" may want to solve a challenge in your life, so your "outer self" needs to take action. First, think about the context of where the challenge is. Then think about who best would give advice about that kind of challenge. Ask for their time. Tell them the challenge, and listen with both ears to their advice. Tell them you're going to really take their advice to heart, and consider how to apply it to your next best steps. Then thank them for their help.

Here are two examples of using your "inner self" and "outer self" to go after what you want.

Example 1: Asking for Advice on How to Kick a Soccer Ball

Your "inner self" wants to learn to kick a soccer ball to score a goal. You get excited and motivated to get better at soccer after watching the United States women's soccer team in the Olympics. You may even say to yourself, "I can do that!"

Your "outer self" starts to put your desire into action. You start to look around for soccer players who can already kick the ball well. You ask for their coaching. You may mess up and feel clumsy at first, but you keep trying it. You may only do it once, then twice, and finally, after lots of attempts and practice, you are starting to kick the ball into the goal.

Example 2: Sharing a Romantic Feeling

You are at home during summer vacation, and your "inner self" can envision or think about doing something that would be exciting and new for you when sharing a romantic feeling. You think about riding your bicycle to the neighborhood way across town to visit a girl or boy that you like. Or you may think about sending a text to a girl or boy you like that makes you nervous and excited at the same time (yes, you can experience two emotions at the same time).

Your "outer self" goes for it! You act upon this idea and experience your feelings! You get the courage to send that text to your friend expressing your romantic feelings, using appropriate language and your own thoughts and words. After you hit "send," you wait and feel fully your excitement, fear, or other emotions— any and all are good to feel. The point is—you did it!

Space for Writing and Drawing

Know Your Inner and Outer Self

Experience 1
Intrinsic Motivation

"Intrinsic motivation" comes from your "inner self." It is your *inner* drive to achieve, accomplish, or reach a desired state. This inner drive may come from instinct, a deep subconscious desire, or a conscious want.

Compare it to "extrinsic motivation," which refers to the *external* forces that move you to act.

You might have an "intrinsic motivation" to run fast, because it feels good to be outside at the park, and you want to move freely in the sunshine. "Extrinsic motivation" would be when your coach tells you to run laps to strengthen the team. Sometimes you can benefit from "extrinsic motivation" to stay on track in the short term, but "intrinsic motivation" is more powerful in getting you what you want in the long term.

Learning occurs constantly and adds to and changes your intrinsic motivations to manifest what you want, in your best self-interest.

Intrinsic motivation helps you pursue an activity for all sorts of good reasons. You might want to pursue an activity to:

- experience pleasurable things in life
- gain skills you consider important
- make ethical and moral choices

For example, if you develop a new belief about the importance of relationships and choose to define yourself by this belief, then you have the intrinsic motivation to develop meaningful relationships that reinforce your belief system.

★

In this experience, you will come up with your *own* positive affirmation to say every day for the next 4 days to reflect what you want. Your phrase can say that you are learning something new about yourself. Take your best shot.

For example, you want to believe that you can dream of what you want and take actions to achieve your dreams. Your phrases could be:
"I can make my dreams come true!"
"I believe in myself!"

Now it is up to you! What do you want to do or experience? What positive affirmation do you want to say?

As you did in a previous experience, you can say it out loud when you are looking at yourself in the mirror, or you can say it when placing your hand over your heart.

Make sure that your positive affirmation reflects what you want. This is all about your unique life, what you want to learn, experience, do, feel, say, and more.

Write your phrase here:

Now say it every day for the next 4 days!

What did it feel like to say your own affirmation?

Space for Writing and Drawing

Know Your Inner and Outer Self

Experience 2
Self-Efficacy

"Self-efficacy" is your belief about your potential and your capacity to grow and learn to become the person you want to become. You believe that you can accomplish a goal or end result and that you are the primary source of your accomplishment.

You can strengthen your self-efficacy by redefining success or failure from a broader perspective. When you think you didn't do well, was that just a thought? Maybe you did better than you thought you did!

You can also strengthen self-efficacy by taking a fresh look at all of your limiting assumptions. An "assumption" is when you suppose you know something, but you never really tested it out to see if it was true for you. For instance, if you think you can't do something, that is just a thought or maybe something somebody told you. If you put the work in, you can do more than you thought you could.

Finally, you can strengthen self-efficacy by understanding your emotions. You may think that something didn't go well, because you felt uncomfortable, or you felt a new emotion you didn't understand. You may have simply made an assumption that a particular emotion was bad, when it was simply different and new.

Thomas Edison, one of the most successful innovators in history, invented most notably the electric lightbulb. He said it took him 10,000 attempts to make a lightbulb. But he didn't fail all those times. He said that he simply discovered 9,999 ways that did not work, and one way that did. He understood self-efficacy!

★

Describe how you took a risk or pressed through when you felt nervous, scared, or upset. Describe how you wanted something and then went on to make it happen in your real life.

Maybe you were really great at what you tried! Hurray!

Or maybe it all "crashed and burned" as the expression goes! In that case, take note of what happened and think about what you want to try differently the next time. Remember, most star athletes have more misses than hits. It's all a part of life! All you have to do to complete this experience is describe when you believed in yourself and took a risk to make something happen.

Know Your Inner and Outer Self

Experience 3
Self-Esteem

You are learning to believe in yourself. You can think about and dream up what you want for now and for your future. You can get the outcomes you want. You can express what you want.

Do you believe that you deserve and can get the feelings associated with being with a close friend and sharing feelings together? You do, and you can!

You learned earlier in the playbook that your "self" consists of all the elements that make you an individual person—your body, mind, emotions, thoughts, sensations, and more.

"Self-esteem" refers to the *value* you place upon all of the elements that make you an individual. If you value all the elements of you, then you have high self-esteem.

Unfortunately, if a teen experiences a parent, teacher, or other important adult as negative, rejecting, or emotionally unavailable and non-supportive, they will construct a view of their "self" as unlovable, incompetent, and generally unworthy. In other words, they develop low self-esteem.

Another source of low self-esteem can come from social media, which sets teens up to compare themselves to others. As you probably already have learned, much of what is posted online can be exaggerated, untrue, or trying to convince you to buy something.

But never fear! You have the heart and the brain power to rebuild your own self-esteem, no matter if you are feeling high or low. You can construct a new view of yourself by noticing and acknowledging your previously unacknowledged strengths. You can see reality, instead of what someone told you.

Teens can get caught up in thinking self-esteem comes *only* from doing well in school, sports, or music. Those are all wonderful things, and you should celebrate all of your successes in those contexts. But this experience focuses on the value you place on your "inner self" and your "outer self."

You can experience positive feelings and value yourself if you really believe in yourself.

Describe how you feel about your "inner self." Think about and write down parts of your "inner self" that you value. It could be your imagination, your hope, your empathy, your ability to feel your emotions, and more. Write about how you appreciate having wants and goals that come from your "inner self." Write about how you deserve to have what you want in life.

Now, think about and write down some parts of your "outer self" that you value. Write about how it felt when you took a risk associated with trying something new; when you courageously did things your way to get what you wanted; or when you gained a sense of confidence when something went better than you thought it would.

Space for Writing and Drawing

Know Your Inner and Outer Self

How Did You Do?

Assess yourself on how you did on this skill. Ask yourself these questions:
- Did you complete all of the experiences for this skill?
- Describe which experience was the most meaningful to you.
- In the space below, draw 1 to 5 stars. Give yourself at least 1 star for completing all the experiences and up to 5 stars if you feel you did great on this skill overall.

Meet with Your Parent

Take a look back at everything you did for this skill and choose something to share with your parent. You can choose to share something you:
- learned about yourself
- are feeling
- created or made
- are doing to flourish and build your optimal mental health
- want to ask your parent about
- want to ask your parent to help you do
- and more

It is up to you to choose what you want to share about this skill. Remember, this is one meeting in your life when it is all about *you*, so you can practice having optimal mental health. There are no right or wrong answers! Your meeting doesn't have to be perfect. Give it a try!

Champions in Life

CERTIFICATE OF ACCOMPLISHMENT

Optimal Mental Health Superstar Award
for Completing Skill 3

Know Your Inner and Outer Self

_____

completed all of the experiences of the
Know Your Inner and Outer Self skill.

Let Your Star Shine!

Skill 4

Connect Mind and Body

How you think and feel impacts your body,
and how you treat your body impacts what you think and feel.

Connect Mind and Body

Your heart beats and you breathe every single second of the day, whether you are sleeping or awake—pretty cool! Your body is always with you!

For optimal mental health, you need to know that your mind and your body have a dynamic connection between them. Your mind and body are in constant communication—literally every second. What you think and feel impacts your body and bodily sensations, while at the same time, your bodily sensations influence your mind and your interpretations.

It is very important as a teen to know and feel this dynamic connection between mind and body, because both are changing faster than they ever have. When you have powerful feelings or new sensations, you can be assured that this is all perfectly normal for a teen. And also, wonderful and amazing!

Your Mind

As you read earlier, your "mind" is that part of you that feels, perceives, thinks, imagines, desires, and remembers. Further, your mind is a biological system that reaches all parts of your body.

You are perpetually in a growth mindset; you are always changing. This is good to recognize, because you can change your circumstances and who you are in your life, a powerful force.

Your mind is shaped by your internal thoughts and feelings, and also by how you choose to interpret external influences such as your family, school, and community.

Your Brain

An important part of the mind is your brain, which has grey and white matter, sits at the top of your head, and connects to your spinal cord. The brain is the main center for receiving and interpreting bodily sensations and for sending information to your muscles and organs.

Your brain connects with your entire body, but it has a really powerful connection with your digestive system and your gut. They actually "talk" to each other. You know the expression: "I have a 'gut' feeling!" Well, you really do! And you have experienced it when your stomach churned before a test, or your stomach flipped happily when you were excited to go to an event.

Emotions, memory, and conscious and subconscious thoughts occur in the brain. Some parts of the brain focus on experiencing sensations. Other parts help you really think about your decisions.

Perhaps the most important brain function is "neuroplasticity," which is the brain's ability to change throughout your life—based upon experiences and the learning that occurs within each experience.

Your brain has 100 billion neurons, which create electrical impulses. When you practice anything—whether you are throwing a baseball, playing an instrument, coding, or learning to observe your feelings and thoughts—the neurons in your brain are wiring together in new ways. You are creating patterns in behavior and thought by connecting different parts of your brain.

Think about this idea further. If you are constantly experiencing new senses, thoughts, body movements, book learning, physical contact, among numerous daily activities, and if your brain is adapting to each new experience, then you are literally changing your brain. You are creating new pathways in your brain constantly. It can be said that who you are now is not who you will be in the future—and certainly not who you were in the past!

Your mind is powerful! If you see yourself as a good person doing good things in the world, your brain will literally create the pathways necessary to think about how to do this, and how to manifest the goodness that you envision.

Physical Movement

Play in your body! Play sports or dance around your room just for fun. This develops your muscles so that you have the strength to do what you want in terms of physical movement. You may have dreams of being an accomplished dancer or athlete in particular sports. This requires higher levels of conditioning and coordination that are within your reach. Even sitting for long hours at your desk studying requires physical stamina so that you can focus upon learning what you want to learn.

Never harm your body, even if you are sad or frustrated, and never let someone else harm your body either. Your body wants to be healthy, with all systems working well together.

Running a Marathon – Mind and Body Working Together

A great example of the mind and body working together is when you have a goal for achieving something physical.

Imagine that you see on television a marathon runner competing in the Boston Marathon. You have limited running experiences, and you don't have the muscle conditioning to even contemplate running in such an event. Yet, you say to yourself, "I can imagine doing this! I can imagine running that far in front of so many people."

Your mind can envision or dream of running, yet your body is not ready to accomplish this, and maybe, you do not even know where to begin. Yikes!

You are good at reading and learning, that is a good start. So, you begin reading about running, and especially distance running, to see what others say about their experiences. You find out that there is much more to this dream than you first thought. Yet, you are not deterred. You have committed yourself to training your mind and body to embark on this seemingly impossible journey.

Through your readings, you learn about the importance of nutrition and the daily conditioning of various and numerous muscle groups, such as legs, core, and arms. Then you realize that there are numerous internal bodily systems that you also need to work on and improve upon, such as the respiratory system, so that you can breathe consistently and increase your capacity to breathe when your body is stressed by physical exertion.

Your "metacognitive" function, which means "thinking about your thinking," makes plans for embarking on your running challenge journey. This kind of thinking occurs in the top front of your brain, a location called the "prefrontal cortex." This part of your brain allows for self-reflection, which is truly and uniquely a human function. It is one of the amazing qualities that makes us human.

As you think about your plans, your "prefrontal cortex" actually starts to form new pathways to the "amygdala," which is in the middle of your brain, and which processes emotions and emotional memories. The connection—between these two parts of the brain—helps you to get over your fears about physical challenges, body image, or self-esteem concerns about whether you have the confidence to achieve in this manner.

Once you experience the joy and happiness associated with small gains in your journey toward manifesting your dream of running, your brain releases both "dopamine" and "endorphins" and the feelings of happiness. These natural, internally-produced chemicals make you feel good, and more importantly, *you* created them!

You connected your mind and body!

Taking Care of Your Body with Healthy Food

As a *Champion in Life*, take care of your body. Give it good nutrition with fruits, vegetables, and protein.

You will want to monitor your digestive system to make certain that you are regular in your bowel movements and going to the bathroom. A healthy body should poop once a day, or maybe more, depending upon what you eat and the levels of stress in your life.

Food is a part of the mind-body connection. Food provides energy for your body. It also provides nutrients, such as vitamins and minerals, that your mind and body need to function.

When it comes to food, simply think: "variety! variety! variety!" In any given week, eat every *color* of food you can think of. If you ate bread, rice, pasta, and potatoes, the color of those foods is "white," which is fine. Now make sure you *also* eat red, orange, yellow, green, and purple (or blue) foods—such as a red apple, orange carrot, yellow squash, green lettuce, and blueberries.

Also, have a mix of *raw* foods and *cooked* foods every week. For example, eat a raw apple and cooked peas. Most of all, your food should have been *alive* at one point. If you have take-out food on one night, then have a home-cooked meal the next night. If you're interested, learn to cook, so you can make dinner for the rest of your family once in a while!

Different people can react to foods differently. Some teens have allergies to gluten (a substance in wheat, bread, and pasta) or to peanuts, as two examples. You may need a special kind of diet in those cases, which you work on together with your parent.

Different foods can actually affect your mood. If you eat too much sugary food, you might get a boost, and then a crash in energy. It is okay to eat cookies and cake once in a while—make them special, and not at every meal.

Rather than focusing on your looks, your weight, or your size, ask yourself, do you have the *energy* to do what you want? Do you want to go to the big game tonight? You'll need good energy to cheer. Do you want to join the dance club? You'll need good energy to dance.

Listen to your body. Which foods give you energy? Which foods drag you down? Above all, eat! Enjoy! You're sending a message to your brain that you *deserve* energy and nutrients. You're worth it!

Puberty and Your Changing Mind and Body

Having optimal mental health doesn't require that your body looks a certain way. Everyone can be a *Champion in Life*!

Your physical body includes amazing features. Everyone's body is different. You have a different height, weight, and hair color than other people. Your skin may be a certain color, or have freckles, or have hair on it.

Your physical body is also made up of internal organs, for example: your esophagus, stomach, intestines, and entire digestive system; your heart, blood, and entire circulatory system; and your nose, lungs, diaphragm, and entire respiratory system. Your muscular system, made up of your heart and skeletal muscles, allow you to move your arms, legs, head, and torso.

You also have "smooth muscles" that work involuntary throughout your body to help keep everything functioning every day, from your reproductive system to going to the bathroom.

Your internal body is exciting: with sensations like an upset stomach when you eat too much candy, a fast heartbeat when you go down a water slide, feeling dizzy when you see a beautiful person that you find attractive, or feeling intensity and sensitivity in your sexual organs—vagina, vulva, and clitoris for a girl, and penis and testicles for a boy.

As a teen, you have already started, or will soon begin "puberty." This is the stage in life when you become capable of producing or bearing children. It is perfectly normal and healthy to begin puberty at different ages; some teens start earlier, and others later.

Your body has always had "hormones," which are chemical messengers that coordinate different functions in your body. The "hormones" that change around puberty begin between ages 8 and 14 and last until the early 20's.

During the teenage years, the sex hormones of "testosterone" and "estrogen" influence your primary and secondary sexual characteristics. While men and women actually have *both* sex hormones, the dominant sex hormone for men is testosterone; for women, estrogen.

These hormones are chemicals in your body that you do not have control over. All that you can do is observe the effects on your bodily changes, psychological moods, and sexual attractions or impulses. Learn what these are telling you and what your body is communicating. It is important to listen, as these changes are basic to all humans, and can tell you about your unique interests and desires, and guide your future relationships.

Everyone changes differently, but in general, most people experience physical changes that take place over several years. For teen boys, testicles may get bigger, and hair grows under the arms, on the face, and around the genitals. Muscles get bigger and stronger.

For teen girls, breasts develop over several years, hair grows in the pubic area and under the arms, and some girls get more curves in their hips. Menstruation begins any time between 9 and 16 years of age. This is a cycle when a girl sheds the lining of her uterus, which is a muscular organ in her pelvis. This cycle is part of the reproductive system, which prepares the body for making a baby when the girl is older and wants to have one. The human body is quite a miracle!

When you have new feelings in your sexual organs, which is absolutely *normal* for everybody going through puberty, you can take appropriate action to relieve these feelings through orgasms achieved through masturbation, self-touch, or other explorations of your body. These are healthy ways to take good care of your body.

The change in the puberty "hormone" levels are substantial, with increases of 10 times the amount of testosterone in boys and estrogen in girls.

For your emotions, these hormones can be like a large infusion of water in a system designed to handle a trickle, like a slow-moving river that suddenly receives 10 inches of rain during a big thunderstorm. It makes the water just that more powerful, so much so that the river can barely hold the amount of water.

So, give yourself a break! Realize that your brain and your body are going through huge changes. But also realize that your brain and body will soon learn how to accommodate the new hormones and figure out how best to handle them.

Changes in your body are normal—to learn more, be proactive and ask your family doctor or people you trust who have been through puberty.

Attraction and Intimacy

One of the most interesting and exciting developments during the teen years is that you start being attracted to other people your age in new ways. Being attracted to other people and wanting to interact in physical ways, such as hugging, kissing, touching hands, or genital stimulation are perfectly normal and healthy. It is a sign of mental health to *want* to engage in physical intimacy.

Of course, physical intimacy requires that you both be on the same page about it, be in the same age group, and have mutual consent and good communication about your feelings and emotions.

This kind of interest develops at a different rate for everyone. Teens will have many physical, mental, and social changes from the beginning of puberty into young adulthood. Learn more about puberty, and always put well-being first.

Attraction and sexuality should always be your own; you can be attracted to whomever you want. And you can identify as a gender or two genders. Your attraction and sexuality are your own inner thoughts and feelings. You will want to express these inner thoughts and feelings with others at the appropriate time and in the appropriate manner.

Attraction can often start with the outside appearance of a body. But remember, people often judge looks through their own kind of lens. This means no matter how nice you look, some people won't notice. They literally can't see you, because their own lens is clouded with their own thoughts and perceptions. It goes for you, too. Maybe you were attracted to someone for how they look, and then you find out they aren't very nice. But then a nice person you hadn't noticed before becomes more attractive to you when you get to know them and see their great inner qualities.

You get to choose when, where, and how to express intimacy and touch. If you are someone's "object," trying to fit only what they want, the relationship is never going to work. You are both equal people, so you should both be getting and receiving the pleasure of caring and attraction. Intimacy of any kind is meant for people who do everything they can to lift each other up, and never put each other down.

If another teen makes fun of you for anything regarding your interest in intimacy, remember that is really because *they* are nervous about growing and changing themselves.

Sex and intimacy are basic human needs; everyone has them. Sex is the physical expression of desire, excitement, or attraction. Intimacy is the inner feeling associated with the physical expression. For example, you may touch someone's hand tenderly and softly, while feeling closeness and "at one" with the other person.

Teens can find it difficult to talk to their parents about puberty, sex, and intimacy, and at the same time, parents can find it difficult to talk to their teens. Press on and learn more by asking them questions, talking to your family doctor, and reading well-researched books on reproduction, birth control, and protecting your health. Always remember that the internet can be filled with false and sensationalized information. The more you know the facts about puberty, attraction, intimacy, and sexuality, the better you will be able to make decisions that enhance your well-being and mental health.

If you are a *Champion* of your physical body, you realize that only you can experience what you're experiencing. Anything you think and feel is okay.

You are growing up! On your own schedule, you are on your way to becoming a wonderful and strong adult—that is something to celebrate!

Connect Mind and Body

Experience 1
Emotions and Sensations

Think about the best thing that happened to your mind *and* body this week and how you felt. It should be something that you felt in your body as a sensation, and also in your mind as an emotion or feeling. Feel deeply. Remember that "self-affect" is the ability to "fully experience your emotions and feelings."

- Were you walking in the rain, and you felt free?
- Maybe you listened to a song and were moved to tears or inspired to think differently about yourself and the world.
- Did you jump up and down when you accomplished something important and meaningful to you?
- Did you learn to do something you never did before, and you felt happy about it?
- What did you feel when you ate a certain food?
- Maybe you wanted to hug your parent, because you were feeling love for them.
- Did you have feelings toward another person, such as attraction, excitement, or passion?

Being in nature can be awe-inspiring and fill up all your senses. You can smell the grass in the fields and the fir trees in the woods. Hear the birds sing. Even if you live in a town or city, you can feel the soft breeze and the sun, and get inspired to write a poem, story, or music. Be inspired to explore your joy.

Further, you might have felt high levels of joy and happiness from the "dopamine" your brain created, because you accomplished something you set out to accomplish.

Name, draw, or represent the *best* thing that happened to your mind and body this week and how you felt. Your drawing can be an "impressionistic" drawing, where it doesn't look like anything, simply colors and lines and whatever you want. Express the feelings you had in your body and mind, whatever that means to you.

Connect Mind and Body

Experience 2
Self-Concept

Your "self-concept" is how you view yourself. "Self-image" and "self-perception" are others ways to say it. You have an image of yourself. You have an image of your body and your mind.

Important references for your "self-concept" can be your interests and activities and what you tend to be good at doing. These interests are usually grouped or categorized, for example: academic, extracurricular, peer groups, friends, intellectual, physical, athletic, musical, artistic, and more.

Self-concept most often develops through becoming aware of your innate strengths and then developing related qualities and characteristics over time.

Healthy self-concept is formed from the inside-out and not from the outside-in. Yet, to fully develop your self-concept, you need to interact with other people. Friends and family help you to see yourself through their views and perceptions. This can help you feel connected through contribution to each other.

But they may also make assumptions about who you are based on past experiences and not who you are becoming. Or maybe they think one part of you is more important, but you actually believe another part is more important.

In sum, you need to construct your self-concept from *two* main sources:

- primarily, your own internal views, truths, values, and strengths

- secondarily, your external interactions with family, friends, community, and the broader culture around you

It is kind of like a dance. The interplay between internal and external views are always moving, and always exciting.

Here is an example. Through reading this book, you are becoming more self-aware; you are starting to understand that self-awareness is interesting and helpful in your life. So, you decide to share some of your experiences with a friend about how self-awareness works.

As you and your friend are on your way to school, a lesson, a sport, or some other activity, you describe something that was meaningful to you. Now imagine that your friend responds with appreciation, and thanks you for this new way of looking at things. Or, your friend says that they experienced something similar, and you hug or laugh.

This moment of connection with your friend releases the positive "dopamine" chemicals in your body. Your mind and whole body feel good! Now you have more energy and motivation. Your body is energized when you are feeling this positive feedback. You had an impact on the context of friendship, making your friendship more meaningful to you. And you have developed an image of yourself as someone who cares and makes a difference with your friends.

In this experience, you will be recalling a time when you took an action. You can choose whether it is something you *did* for someone as a physical act, or whether it was something you *shared* with someone as words or feelings.

Your action was based on your own sense of "self," when you contributed ideas and feelings from your "inner self" and brought them to others through your "outer self." In taking the action, you received feedback about what you did or said from another person or multiple people.

Here are some examples of what you might have chosen to *do, say, or share*, along with some different kinds of feedback you might have received to affirm your self-expression.

- Play an instrument, and people clap.
- Run fast, and win a medal.
- Lift a heavy weight, and your friends are impressed.
- Hit a softball, and everyone jumps up and down when you win the game.

- Make a delicious and healthy sandwich for a brother and sister, and they have the energy to play.
- Babysit for your brothers and sisters or another family, and they appreciate you with a "thank you."
- Style your friend's hair, and they look awesome.
- Share something you learned about yourself with your friend, and they say they can really relate to it in their own life.
- Share a real feeling, and have a special moment with someone.
- Tell someone you want to learn to do something, and they happily show you how to do it.
- And more . . .

Now describe or make a drawing that represents what you did, said, or shared. Then, describe the form of feedback you received from other people, whether it was spoken or shown in some other way. Finally, describe how you felt when you received the feedback, and how you used the feedback, no matter what it was, to really lift up, affirm, and shape your self-concept.

Space for Writing and Drawing

Connect Mind and Body

Experience 3
Self-Esteem and Your Body

External and cultural forces can impact you and shape your inner feelings or perspectives about your "self-esteem." As you learned earlier, self-esteem is the *value* you place on your qualities and characters.

When it comes to your body during the teen years, these external forces can really have a big effect on your self-esteem. You can really get caught up in how you look in comparison to others.

It is almost impossible not to notice when the image of someone on the internet or social media looks beautiful. First, know that it is okay to appreciate when something or someone looks beautiful. The next step is to be aware of the context—is the image staged, air-brushed, or altered by artificial intelligence? The final step is to shift from comparing yourself to going for something you want to *do* or *feel*.

For example, you see an image of a music idol that you love. They look gorgeous and alive in the image. You may start to compare looks. It is normal to compare; you almost can't stop yourself!

But here is how to turn it around. Ask yourself, is the image doing something you want to *do* or *feel* but haven't had the chance to do yet?

So now, begin to focus on whether the image puts out a feeling that you want to experience. Think of ways you can experience that feeling in your mind and body. Put on the music idol's songs or go to their concert with friends. When the idol puts on an amazing performance, go wild! Jump, dance, and feel great! Feel inside that you are a beautiful, amazing, and alive person!

Another way to gain self-esteem is to really listen for those moments in life when someone appreciates you. Maybe someone you are attracted to takes a second look at you! Wow! Or maybe someone you are attracted to actually doesn't really notice you (sad face!), but because you dressed extra nice, your friends really appreciate how beautiful or handsome you look today (happy face!). You feel valued by yourself and your peers. You looked your best!

For this experience, choose one of these two actions. Or do *both*!

1. Look your best today, just because. Love your body, just because. You don't have to be going someplace special, or doing it because you want to look good for someone else, but that's okay too. Wash and style your hair. Put on your favorite clothes. Wear some perfume or cologne. Put a great smile on your face. You're looking really good! Now celebrate how great you look by just feeling good about yourself. Or, take a selfie, go out with friends, or go to an event. The main thing is to take loving care of your body! Send a message to your body that you care about yourself, just as you are!

2. Describe, draw, or create an image of a time when you were looking and feeling beautiful or handsome, inside and out! As always, your drawing can be "impressionistic," where it is more about the lines and colors that represent how you feel inside, rather than having to look exactly like a human figure. The key here is, if you felt it once, you can feel it again! Feel yourself looking awesome, inside and out!

Space for Writing and Drawing

Space for Writing and Drawing

Connect Mind and Body

How Did You Do?

Assess yourself on how you did on this skill. Ask yourself these questions:
- Did you complete all of the experiences for this skill?
- Describe which experience was the most meaningful to you.
- In the space below, draw 1 to 5 stars. Give yourself at least 1 star for completing all the experiences and up to 5 stars if you feel you did great on this skill overall.

Meet with Your Parent

Take a look back at everything you did for this skill and choose something to share with your parent. You can choose to share something you:
- learned about yourself
- are feeling
- created or made
- are doing to flourish and build your optimal mental health
- want to ask your parent about
- want to ask your parent to help you do
- and more

It is up to you to choose what you want to share about this skill. Remember, this is one meeting in your life when it is all about *you*, so you can practice having optimal mental health. There are no right or wrong answers! Your meeting doesn't have to be perfect. Give it a try!

Suggestion: Ask your parent their personal views about sex and intimacy, such as when they first felt feelings toward one another, how to think about appropriate sexual relations, and how you, as a teen, might support these in yourself.

Champions in Life

CERTIFICATE OF ACCOMPLISHMENT

Optimal Mental Health Superstar Award
for Completing Skill 4

Connect Mind and Body

---

completed all of the experiences of the
Connect Mind and Body skill.

Let Your Star Shine!

Skill 5

Dream Big Dreams

Let your imagination soar!
Dream big dreams for your future feelings and experiences.

Dream Big Dreams

To dream is to have a strong desire for something purposeful, beautiful, and wonderful. Dreaming *big* dreams means you can see or imagine something that doesn't exist yet. You can dream of a magnificent future state of being.

A big dream is a vision magnified many, many times over. Having a vision is not about eyesight. You have a vision when you use your "mind's eye," or what you can see in your imagination.

Dreaming big dreams shapes your future and who you will become. Yes, that is the power of your dreams! Dreaming big dreams is courageous and exciting. It is also a sign of optimal mental health. Dreaming big dreams is something teens are very, very good at.

People often stop dreaming big dreams as they get older and no longer think something is possible. But teens are great at dreaming.

Keep your dreams! All the feelings and thoughts you have when you dream big dreams are really healthy for your mind. You are experiencing your imagination. You are building your sense of hope.

People create their futures. Many people plod along day after day, living as if they are simply playing out roles in a play that is already written. But that play has *not* been written. You must create it through a vision of your ideal future.

Design your own destiny by dreaming of what your life can be. A clear understanding of your dreams answers two questions:

- "What will I be doing?" (activities)
- "What will I feel like?" (energy)

It is usually easy to imagine what you will be *doing*—the activities and tasks you will be doing and the success you will be enjoying from doing those tasks.

It is sometimes more difficult to imagine what you will be *feeling*—your energy, personal emotions, behaviors, attitudes, and character traits you will be living by in order to produce the results you want.

When you dream big dreams, you see what is possible for you, your friends, siblings, family, community, and even the world. You see what is possible for your contributions and accomplishments.

When formulating your dreams, do not ask, "Is this realistic?" for you are creating your own destiny, and you will decide if your dreams become a reality or not.

Walt Disney, the inventor of Disney World and all of those wonderful characters and movies, asserted, "If you can dream it, you can do it."

Understand and believe in your dreams so they can guide your life choices and propel you toward your future self. Your dream can help you to reach those who need your sense of your calling, or why you think you are here in the world at this time. Your dream can help you design life and career strategies that communicate your self-awareness and your vision for a better life and world.

Getting clearer about your dreams can even take the pressure off of trying to be perfect for everybody. You can be more focused on what is most meaningful to you. You can "prioritize"—which means rank or arrange in order of importance—the activities that best support your dreams.

For *Champions in Life*, a vision is not really about having material *things*, but more about having *experiences* and *feelings*. It is fine to say you envision buying a video game, shoes, or a car. But that is not really the kind of vision that the playbook emphasizes for optimal mental health. Having a vision is more than having a goal, because it has more feeling to it.

You can have a vision about an experience, for example, "My vision is to . . .
. . . catch a baseball when my friend throws it to me."
. . . draw a picture of my favorite animal."
. . . plant a beautiful garden."

You can have a vision about a feeling, for example, "My vision is to . . .
. . . feel really safe and comfortable when I wrap myself in a big soft blanket."
. . . feel love for my parents when they talk with me about me and my life."
. . . have friends who really care about me, and I care about them."

When your vision includes other people, remember that you can never really control other people, nor can you see inside their thoughts. You can only put it out there, so they can make their own choice to connect back to you.

Having a vision means you might not even know yet how you are going to make it happen. For example, if you have been feeling sad lately about anything, your vision can be that you feel more moments of real happiness and joy throughout your day, and then take the appropriate actions to make those feelings a reality.

To Dream the Impossible Dream

The most powerful kind of dream is one that sounds impossible.

Your dream is so big that if you told someone, they may laugh and say, "that's impossible!"

Instead of listening to that negative voice, read this quote for inspiration:

You see things; and you say, "Why?"
But I dream things that never were; and I say, "Why not?"
—George Bernard Shaw

It is extremely good for your mental health to allow yourself to dream big, impossible dreams. This is the opportunity to dream up something really amazing, something that seems impossible.

Use what you are really feeling to imagine your impossible dream. For example, "My big, impossible dream is that . . .
. . . people stop being mean to each other."
. . . every corner of the planet has fresh water and clear air."
. . . teens everywhere in the world feel inner peace and unconditional love."

As you can clearly see, this kind of impossible dream probably won't be accomplished during the time you complete this playbook. But can you surely come up with steps along the way to the impossible dream.

For example, if you envision that everyone in the world stops being mean to each other, you can begin by feeling more love in your own life, noticing when people are kind to you, and thanking them for that. Or if someone is mean, you can come up with a plan to not believe everything they say and get support to build yourself up so their meanness just bounces right off of you.

For another example, if you envision every corner of the planet having fresh water and clear air, propose a new recycling program at school, or plant a butterfly garden with your family. You and your friends can take a walk in nature and draw pictures of how you feel about all the beauty around you.

What if you are feeling overwhelmed with this idea of even having this kind of impossible dream? Simply take a step back and look at things differently. Maybe your dream is to not be so overwhelmed by things that seem out of your reach, and to know that it is okay to fail at things. Your dream may be to know that even if you don't achieve something right away, you have learned a lesson to help you achieve it the next time.

There are five phases to pursuing an impossible dream.

- First, dream it! Let yourself go and feel something that would be amazing.

- Second, decide when and if it is time to share it. You may need to keep your impossible dream to yourself for a while, so you don't expend all of your energy trying to explain or defend it to other people. This will give you the time and space to envision all the wonderful details of your dream.

- Third, come up with a vision for a step along the way. For example, if you want to take a step towards a kinder world, take a simple action to thank people when they are kind to you and others.

- Fourth, at the appropriate moment, you will probably need to share your vision for one of your steps along the way. The reason is that for most projects, you will need partners to do and make things with you. For example, if you envision planting a butterfly garden as a step towards a clean and healthy environment, you will need to ask other people to help you plant the garden.

- Fifth, acknowledge yourself for your accomplishment and for moving in the direction of your dream.

You may have heard the expression, "Aim for the stars, or you will never know how far you can go!" Your impossible dream will take you far in life. It is the kind of dream that will take a lifetime to accomplish, and it will include all of your hopes for a better world.

Dream Big Dreams

Experience 1
Health

When you have a vision for your future life, begin with your mental and physical health. They are truly important!

Describe your vision for feelings and experiences in the area of your health and well-being.

My vision for my mental health is:

My vision for my physical health is:

Space for Writing and Drawing

Dream Big Dreams

Experience 2
Inspiration and Hope

Just like dreams, inspiration and hope involve a vision of a future state, including all circumstances and emotions that are meaningful and move you. They are what you can see in your mind's eye.

"Inspiration" is the spark or seed of an idea of a desired future state. Your inspiration can come either from another person, from your inner life, or your life experience.

"Hope" is the belief and feeling that something you envision will happen. You hope you can manifest your dream. Hopeful thought reflects the belief that you can and will pursue your dreams, and that you can manifest your unique life purpose.

Hopeful people see the future as better than the present, and believe they have the power to make positive change. If you are hopeful, you are energetic and full of life. You will be able to develop strategies to manifest your dreams and plan contingencies in the event that you are faced with problems along the way.

Obstacles are viewed as challenges to overcome and are bypassed by garnering support and implementing alternative pathways. Perceiving the likelihood of good outcomes, you focus on success, and you experience more positive feelings and less distress.

Generally, if you have high hopes, you experience less anxiety and less stress specific to making positive change happen. So, you can be in the present moment more fully, even as you hope for the future.

★

Describe a time you felt inspired and hopeful at the same time. Someone or something inspired you to believe something was possible, and you were hopeful that it was going to happen. Pick a time when your inspiration and hope led to something great. For example, describe a time when you were inspired to try out for a team, you had high hopes, and you made the team! Or perhaps you were inspired to ask someone to go to a dance, you had high hopes for a positive response, and the person said "yes!"

If you find it more compelling, then you can choose instead to write a poem or short story about what inspiration and hope feel like. Let yourself believe anything is possible!

Space for Writing and Drawing

Space for Writing and Drawing

Dream Big Dreams

Experience 3
Dream and Flourish

Earlier in the playbook, you learned that "flourishing" means to go after your highest dreams, pursue more than the ordinary, move in the direction of new possibilities, and define for yourself what is really awesome. You had the opportunity earlier to describe flourishing in a specific context you chose.

Now it is time to consider your dream for flourishing in your entire life, and not just one context. Include the big dreams that sound impossible.

In this experience, you will imagine your vision for your best, most flourishing life. Make it the highest vision possible. Your vision needs to be about you. Consider your hopes and fears. Consider what is important to you. Even if you have doubts, even if you're afraid that you can't do it, envision what is possible, your personal best.

To get started, finish these thoughts:

"My vision for my flourishing life is . . ."
"My vision of a good person is . . ."
"My vision for the type of person that I will become is . . ."

All of these thoughts make up your personal vision for your life. Anything is possible for you, because you were born with a creative imagination. Influential psychologist Carl Jung said, "I am not what happens to me. I am what I choose to become."

There are no right or wrong answers! Give yourself the space to really enjoy this experience.

★

Describe, draw, or create something to represent your big dreams for your life. Remember, you can always use other sheets of paper, or other forms of creativity.

To give yourself lots of space, create a "Dream and Flourish Board"—a bulletin board with images, photos, and drawings pinned to it of everything that you envision for your life. Include your big dreams for yourself, for others, and for everyone. Include how you will feel inside. Include your big, impossible dreams, too. Go for it!

Space for Writing and Drawing

Space for Writing and Drawing

Dream Big Dreams

How Did You Do?

Assess yourself on how you did on this skill. Ask yourself these questions:
- Did you complete all of the experiences for this skill?
- Describe which experience was the most meaningful to you.
- In the space below, draw 1 to 5 stars. Give yourself at least 1 star for completing all the experiences and up to 5 stars if you feel you did great on this skill overall.

Meet with Your Parent

Take a look back at everything you did for this skill and choose something to share with your parent. You can choose to share something you:
- learned about yourself
- are feeling
- created or made
- are doing to flourish and build your optimal mental health
- want to ask your parent about
- want to ask your parent to help you do
- and more

It is up to you to choose what you want to share about this skill. Remember, this is one meeting in your life when it is all about *you*, so you can practice having optimal mental health. There are no right or wrong answers! Your meeting doesn't have to be perfect. Give it a try!

Champions in Life

CERTIFICATE OF ACCOMPLISHMENT

Optimal Mental Health Superstar Award
for Completing Skill 5

Dream Big Dreams

_____

completed all of the experiences of the Dream Big Dreams skill.

Let Your Star Shine!

Skill 6

Discover Your Purpose

Discover moments every day when you make a difference.
Continue to discover your purpose throughout your life.

Discover Your Purpose

At a very basic level, "purpose" is your intention in any given situation or context. It is when you assign *meaning* to a particular event and the potential outcome or result from that event. For example, "My purpose (or intention) for cooking is to create something delicious to eat."

In this playbook, purpose is defined more significantly as your intention that you apply to your *entire* life. For example, "My purpose in life is to nurture the health and well-being of people and contribute to their vitality, so when I cook, I choose healthy and nutritious foods to serve the people I love."

It is never too young to start discovering your purpose. You continue to discover your purpose each day, the difference you make just being alive, just being you. Everybody has a purpose. Your purpose is working through you, even if you do not know it yet, and even when it doesn't feel like it. And your purpose can change throughout your life.

Sometimes people mistake "purpose in life" for an occupation or a job. Purpose and occupation are actually different. Your occupation can *support* your purpose, but it is *not* your purpose. For example, you could be a *chef* who nurtures health and well-being. Or you could be a *nurse* who also nurtures health and well-being. Different job, similar purpose.

Other times people turn purpose into a big pressure or stress that you have to figure out right away. But the emphasis should be on the act of *discovering*. Your purpose in life doesn't have to follow a perfect path. There is no test. No job interview. And you discover new aspects of your purpose throughout your life. Purpose is bigger, stronger, and more essential than any schooling, job, or career.

To discover your purpose now and throughout your lifetime, you can use different approaches at different times. Here are some types of questions you can ask yourself to begin to discover your purpose:

1. What do your friends or family frequently thank you for?

2. When did you feel like you did something really great for somebody, but you didn't even need to be recognized or thanked? It simply felt good to do it.

3. When do you light up inside, feel like yourself, feel hopeful and free?

4. Consider your dreams for the life you want to live and the world you want to create. Honor your dreams. They give you insights into what moves, motivates, and inspires you.

5. Think about what issues and concerns in the world you are drawn to, that are important to you, which evoke strong emotions.

6. Do you have an urge to perform a service for others, such as protect them, make them laugh, give them comfort, help them thrive, or many others?

Your life's experiences will speak to you when you are open to listening for what your purpose might be.

Your life purpose is part of the underlying motivation and driving force which guides your actions and brings happiness and fulfillment. Purpose is what you commit your life to, something bigger than yourself, using your unique talents, values, and vision. Your purpose engages a lifelong process that you can continue to discover and improve upon, and it compels you to make a difference in your life, the lives of others, and the condition of the world.

As you discover your purpose throughout your life, it will help guide your personal development, optimal mental health and well-being, friendships, romantic and family relationships, academic studies, and career direction. It will help you to design a life course strategy that communicates your self-awareness and the difference you would like to make in the world.

The following famous quote from George Bernard Shaw, a novelist and dramatist, characterizes life purpose:

This is the true joy in life, the being used for a purpose recognized by yourself as a mighty one; the being a force of nature instead of a feverish selfish little clod of ailments and grievances

complaining that the world will not devote itself to making you happy. I want to be thoroughly used up when I die, for the harder I work the more I live. I rejoice in life for its own sake. Life is no 'brief candle' to me. It is a sort of splendid torch which I have got hold of for the moment, and I want to make it burn as brightly as possible before handing it on to future generations.
—George Bernard Shaw, *Man and Superman*

Purpose connects to spirituality. Your purpose is the reason why you are here, for your existence. It is your *raison d'être* (which means your "reason for being"). Listen to your deepest self, your deepest integrity. Your soul will guide you to know your God-given purpose.

When you are really listening to your soul, you may feel a divine connection, a calling to something higher. This calling can be spiritual in nature and involve a connection with a higher power, an uplifting and transcending force, or feeling of need. You may feel the calling to contribute to the human condition in some way, unique to you and your life experiences and views of a better world and the greater good.

Religion and spirituality are great things to talk about with your parents. People throughout the world have many different kinds of beliefs and religions. It is mind-blowing how many different religious beliefs people have!

Recent scientific discoveries even say that every bit of matter in the universe is in you, and that there is really no actual physical separation between you and the rest of the universe. As if that even makes sense! Another mind-blowing thought! And a pretty spiritual one, too!

As a teen exploring your own beliefs, *never* feel guilty about where you are at on your own spiritual journey. *No one* has the right to put you down for any aspect of your spirituality. You are fine the way you are, now and always, no matter what you do or don't believe. If you exist here in the world, then you *belong*, no matter what anyone else believes. You are loved just as you are.

Discover Your Purpose

Experience 1
Purpose Statement

Everyone has a unique purpose. A "purpose statement" is a one-sentence summary of the difference you make for others in your life. It is always stated as if you are doing it right now.

You will most likely not be clear the first pass or attempt to write your purpose statement. It may take a number of attempts. As you sit with this essential skill and go on living daily life, notice what your soul is communicating to you. Notice what emerges, what you are thinking and feeling.

Remember, this statement is what you are experiencing and feeling at this time in your life. This does *not* have to be your final statement for the rest of your life!

If you really don't know what your purpose statement is, and you are feeling kind of overwhelmed, simply *make one up*, as if you *did* know! The experience is to practice writing a purpose statement, so you can begin to discover your purpose.

You get to benefit from your purpose, too. If you want kindness in the world, you can start by being kind to yourself. When you think about your purpose statement, think about contributing to "self," "other," and "all."

Examples of purpose statements:

- I take positive actions that impact the mental and physical health of people and all humankind.
- I bring moments of awe, hope, and inspiration into my life and the lives of those around me.
- I create a world where it is easier for people to love one another.
- I help myself and others feel better about themselves and know they matter.
- I build things that make life more beautiful for everyone.
- I help people understand context so they can be effective in life.

- I share my feelings so that others are inspired to be more emotionally aware of their own feelings.

Write your one-sentence purpose statement for your life. To get started, answer these questions:

"What do I *want* to give to people?"
"What do I *like* to give to people?"
"What do I feel *called* to give to people and the world?"

Discover Your Purpose

Experience 2
Self-Understanding

You are different than anyone else on this planet. No other person—now, in the past, or in the future—has your unique purpose—no one ever—it is uniquely your own. Other people may have a *similar* purpose, but because you have unique thoughts and feelings, and unique life circumstances, your purpose will manifest in different ways.

In the playbook, "self-understanding" is when you see how your unique purpose comes out every day. Self-understanding is more than being aware of your thoughts and feelings. It is being clear about how your purpose is *unique and different*.

To experience your unique purpose and how you are different than anyone else, think about where in your life you are talented, skilled, or have the abilities to make an impact. Examples could be:

- in your school setting and your ability to deflect the bullying behaviors among your classmates

- how you bring more inspiration to your family members by doing projects together that you feel are important

- in your community to help those less fortunate than you are, by starting a food drive in your neighborhood or a peer-to-peer counseling program in your school

In this experience, you will choose to do two actions this week that demonstrate your purpose. Refer to your purpose statement as a reminder.

If your purpose is "to live with aliveness and vitality and experience everything fully," then ask yourself, "What can I do that demonstrates this?" For example, the two actions you can do this week are:

1. Let yourself feel really happy when you have a moment to yourself, because you are feeling love for who you are and who you are becoming.

2. Notice and name positive sensations you had, such as feeling the sun on your face or delighting in singing your favorite songs.

If your purpose is to "create a world where it is easier for people to love one another," then you might choose to:

1. Tell someone that you think they are great, and do something nice for them for no reason at all.

2. Think of ways to help teach someone how to make positive changes in their life, so they can be inspired by your example.

Describe the two actions you did this week that demonstrated your purpose. Then describe the emotions you felt when you did the actions.

Space for Writing and Drawing

Space for Writing and Drawing

Discover Your Purpose

Experience 3
Soul

Your "soul" is your essence, your basic way of being, and how you connect to your highest purpose. It is difficult to put words to your soul; it is a spiritual connection to a higher power or to the entire universe.

In the playbook, the soul refers to your "inner self" and vital processes such as hope, inspiration, character, integrity, and spirituality. Your soul also includes unrecognized emotions that guide your conscious mind toward a higher purpose.

When you consider all of the parts of the "self," and how all of them are integrated into a whole, you start to get what a soul is.

For the American philosopher Henry David Thoreau, the forest is where he found a soul connection to a higher spiritual force, a feeling of being at one with his surroundings.

In the classic movie *Chariots of Fire,* the lead character Eric Liddell stated, "When I run, I feel God's pleasure." He was discovering and expressing his soul through running. Your soul is your own sense of your higher calling and why you are here.

Another source of finding out about your soul is to make an impact with another person, to help them in some manner. Then reflect upon how you felt. Was it like you were doing good in the world? Did you feel an uplifting spiritual force working through you?

Create something that reflects your soul, then reflect on how this expression of your soul aligns with your purpose.

Draw a picture. Invent a dance. Write music. Produce a video. Write a prayer. Sing a song. Help another person with a project you create. Arrange flowers. Whatever you feel like! Connect your inner beauty and power with the world, because you can do no other. Your soul is more powerful than either your mind or body separately. Listen to your soul's message and honor it. Feel uplifted! This is *not* the time to analyze or judge. Just feel! It is natural to feel this way!

Space for Writing and Drawing

Space for Writing and Drawing

Discover Your Purpose

How Did You Do?

Assess yourself on how you did on this skill. Ask yourself these questions:

- Did you complete all of the experiences for this skill?
- Describe which experience was the most meaningful to you.
- In the space below, draw 1 to 5 stars. Give yourself at least 1 star for completing all the experiences and up to 5 stars if you feel you did great on this skill overall.

Meet with Your Parent

Take a look back at everything you did for this skill and choose something to share with your parent. You can choose to share something you:

- learned about yourself
- are feeling
- created or made
- are doing to flourish and build your optimal mental health
- want to ask your parent about
- want to ask your parent to help you do
- and more

It is up to you to choose what you want to share about this skill. Remember, this is one meeting in your life when it is all about *you*, so you can practice having optimal mental health. There are no right or wrong answers! Your meeting doesn't have to be perfect. Give it a try!

Suggestion: Ask your parent if they want to share with you their own sense of life purpose. You might also ask your parent about their beliefs in religion and spirituality—or their sense of connection to the universe and everything in it.

Champions in Life

CERTIFICATE OF ACCOMPLISHMENT

Optimal Mental Health Superstar Award
for Completing Skill 6

Discover Your Purpose

completed all of the experiences of the
Discover Your Purpose skill.

Let Your Star Shine!

Skill 7

Commit

Commit to demonstrate who you are and what you will do by keeping your word and taking action.

Commit

When you "commit," you make a pledge or a promise. When you commit to doing something, you actually *do* it!

Putting your commitment into action is challenging. For example, if you commit to accomplishing something, you might not get the hang of it at first or succeed for quite some time. This applies to learning a musical instrument, drawing a picture, cooking a meal, playing a sport, and more. When you commit, you keep going even when it all feels awkward and messy. You keep going until you start to see some results.

Commitment is the triumph of possibility over resignation. Commitment is creating your life's destiny versus having it determined for you by others. Your commitments empower you to step beyond what is comfortable or predictable, beyond the limits you thought you had—toward a dynamic and challenging life of active contribution and self-expression.

When determining your set of commitments, do not ask, "Will my commitments help me become famous?" Instead ask, "Will my commitments help me manifest my big dreams and my life purpose? And will my commitments help me reach my dreams for a flourishing life, filled with optimal mental health and well-being?"

Your commitment represents your own deeply held beliefs, regardless of the support of others. The choices you make in your life demonstrate, outwardly, the expressions of your inner beliefs.

Just as your purpose guides your life choices, commitment does as well. Your commitments are expressed in every communication and action, in every part of your life. When you commit—and take action to match your commitment—you will learn more about your personal characteristics and strengths, mental health and well-being, relationships, academics, career direction, and more. Expressing your commitments can make your vision a reality.

Champions in Life know that making a commitment is a powerful thing to do. Commitment makes you strong. Commitment puts you in control of your life. People know who you are by what you are committed to. Commitment takes bravery, as poet Amanda Gorman writes:

There is always light, if only we're brave enough to see it.
If only we're brave enough to be it.
—Amanda Gorman

Space for Writing and Drawing

Commit

Experience 1
Beliefs

All of your thoughts and actions have underlying beliefs, even if you are not aware of these. Your beliefs shape your thoughts, actions, and commitments. The playbook already mentioned spiritual beliefs. But there are other kinds of beliefs.

You have also formed beliefs about your abilities, your value as a person, your family culture, your community, and how the world works. Some of those beliefs can actually limit what you think is possible. Beliefs can change throughout your life as you test them out and see what really works for you.

If you are not aware of your beliefs, then reflect upon your recent thoughts and actions. They will tell you what you believe about yourself, others, and the world.

Often, you are not aware of your beliefs, especially those that are uniquely your own. As a teen, most of your beliefs are embedded or enmeshed with those of your family, friends, school, or community.

It is perfectly okay to have your *own* beliefs. In fact, it is essential to have self-understanding, and to be free to choose your own "self" and your own life course.

This experience is intended to help you uncover and declare your own beliefs about who you are now and about your trajectory for your future.

Answer these questions:

- What are your own beliefs that bring you positive feelings, joy, energy, motivation, action, and self-esteem?

- When you look at your life, what do you know are your beliefs?

- What would you like to think your beliefs are?

- How are these beliefs similar or different from your parents, siblings, and friends?

Commit

Experience 2
Identity and Integrity

This experience asks you to complete a real *project* of your own design and choice. Take on the challenge!

The project should align your "identity" with your "integrity."

Teens are in a phase in life when they need to develop their own ways of thinking and feeling so they can create their own "identity." Identity is who you *define* yourself to be—who you present yourself to be.

Further, identity is the set of behavioral or personal traits by which you are recognizable to yourself and others. Identity can be experienced as a feeling of being at home in your body and having a sense of knowing where you are going.

People often mistakenly think identity is unchanging, however, all people form and reform their identities over the course of a lifetime and at different and distinct stages of development.

A teen who honors their commitments has "integrity." Your commitments are the words and actions that demonstrate who you are and what you will do.

Integrity is achieved when there is an alignment among your identity, dreams, purpose, and commitments—and when your approaches to achieving these align with the results that show up in your day-to-day reality.

Integrity is shaped through life experiences. You have integrity when you do what you say you are going to do. When you are not able to do what you said you would do, you make things right the next time.

When you honor your commitments, as a part of your whole "self," you will naturally feel good and have increased self-esteem.

Choose a project that represents your identity, integrity, and commitments. Make it a project that you can either complete, or show real progress in your efforts, within one week.

Some examples of projects for which you could show real progress in one week:

- Work with other students at your school to start a recycling program.
- Start a clothing drive for your community.
- Get involved with a national teen mental health program.
- Start a peer-to-peer music therapy program.

Describe your project. Align your project with your dreams, purpose, and commitments.

Next, with integrity, do your project in full, or show some real progress. Demonstrate what a committed person you are!

Finally, turn to the next experience (Commit: Experience 3) to describe how the project progressed or turned out and how you felt about it.

Space for Writing and Drawing

Space for Writing and Drawing

Commit

Experience 3
Happiness

This experience is a reflection on the project you completed in Experience 2. It requires that you produced some results. The results can be awesome; or, they can be a step along the way toward awesome.

If by chance you did not produce any results that mean anything to you (it happens!), or if you think the project just didn't seem to go very well, then simply choose another project and do Experience 2 again. Maybe for the second project, ask your parent for suggestions. Or reconsider whether you are being too hard on yourself, and come up with some meaningful results that maybe you hadn't thought of at first. You'll get there!

This experience is all about recognizing that when you take a risk, commit to a project that is important to *you*, complete it, and then reflect on the results, you can generate some wonderful feelings.

Those wonderful feelings include "happiness" and "satisfaction."

"Happiness" is an emotion of pleasure, contentment, elation, joy, a feeling all is well, or all of these. Happiness is an experience and a conscious thought.

There is no absolute state of happiness. It is an interpretation of an experience that makes you happy.

Happiness can light upon you at any time. When you are grateful, or relaxed, or loved, you can feel very happy. Those moments are awesome!

On the other hand, an old expression says, "You're about as happy as you make up your mind to be." So, it is often said happiness is a choice.

This experience is about the kind of happiness that comes from taking action to make something happen and then feeling the "satisfaction"—or pleasure and contentment—that you made it happen or worked with others to make it happen.

The happiness that feels like satisfaction reflects that a deep want has been realized. This deep want may be a conscious thought or an intuitive desire. Satisfaction comes with evidence that a want, desire, or intended result has been realized or manifest.

Happiness and satisfaction occur when the resulting circumstances in your life match your dreams and commitments for your life, after taking action to implement a strategy to produce results.

You can feel good about yourself and your life, when the outcomes that you produce align with your dreams, purpose, and commitments.

Now it is time to reflect on the results you produced from the project in Experience 2. Learning to recognize your results helps to build optimal mental health.

What results did you produce? For example, your clothing drive has been scheduled, and you have recruited volunteers to help.

If the voice inside your head says something about not doing good enough, simply say, "Save your critique for later! I'm doing something else now!" Then go on to describe the progress you have made.

Last, but certainly not least, describe what you feel when you reflect upon your results. Do you feel satisfaction, joy, contentment, other positive emotions?

Space for Writing and Drawing

Space for Writing and Drawing

Commit

How Did You Do?

Assess yourself on how you did on this skill. Ask yourself these questions:

- Did you complete all of the experiences for this skill?
- Describe which experience was the most meaningful to you.
- In the space below, draw 1 to 5 stars. Give yourself at least 1 star for completing all the experiences and up to 5 stars if you feel you did great on this skill overall.

Meet with Your Parent

Take a look back at everything you did for this skill and choose something to share with your parent. You can choose to share something you:

- learned about yourself
- are feeling
- created or made
- are doing to flourish and build your optimal mental health
- want to ask your parent about
- want to ask your parent to help you do
- and more

It is up to you to choose what you want to share about this skill. Remember, this is one meeting in your life when it is all about *you*, so you can practice having optimal mental health. There are no right or wrong answers! Your meeting doesn't have to be perfect. Give it a try!

Champions in Life

CERTIFICATE OF ACCOMPLISHMENT

Optimal Mental Health Superstar Award
for Completing Skill 7

Commit

_____
completed all of the experiences of the Commit skill.

Let Your Star Shine!

Skill 8

Communicate

Communicate to move the action forward in really positive ways.

Communicate

When you communicate, you talk, sign, gesture, make faces, dance, sing, and more. The best way to communicate is to simply be yourself. You are great the way you are!

Remember how important what you say is. A well-known expression says, "Honor your word as your 'self'!"

When you shape your communication, you are shaping who you are.

If you spend any time on social media, you certainly know that many, many people spend too much time expressing an "opinion," which is an unproven judgement about someone or something. Opinions are fine, but they don't have anything to back them up.

For example, someone may say something ridiculous, such as, "People who wear blue socks can't run very fast." That's so clearly silly, you can just brush that off.

But you can sometimes hear an opinion, and it sounds so convincing, that it begins to sound like a statement of fact. It might even sting. So, if someone says, "People who wear blue socks have poor taste," it can be hurtful, especially if you happen to be wearing blue socks that day. But it is still just an opinion that doesn't change a thing.

People use all kinds of negative communication, such as blaming, taunting, acting like they don't care, or yelling in a blast of anger. All of these negative forms of communication usually stem from that person's poor self-esteem, their attempts to avoid their own pain, or some anger that was modeled in their family.

But never fear! There are lots of types of communication that move the action forward for you and the other people in your life in really positive ways. Focus your attention on these positive forms of communication, and ignore the negative kinds of communication.

These positive communications—such as making a promise—are really strong and powerful. Listening with your whole "self" is also a kind of communication. When you are a good communicator, you are courageous and creative.

Four Important Kinds of Communication

The following four kinds of communication can be useful and help move the action forward in your life. For each kind of communication, read the examples:

Share a Feeling
Sharing a feeling helps you feel more connected, and gives other people permission to be more open.

- I feel frustrated, because I have big dreams, and it seems to take so long to get there!
- Sometimes I can't even name my feelings, and that can be scary.
- Sometimes people are mean, and that feels bad.
- I feel so happy!

Make a Request
Making a request helps to put your commitments into action since many activities in life require help from other people.

- Will you please do my favorite activity with me?
- Please pick me up from the game tomorrow afternoon.
- Would you please help me with this question?
- Please give me a hug!

Make a Promise
Making a promise informs and assures other people that you will do something you said you will do.

- I promise to clean my room before going to school.

- When I get home from school, I promise to tell you one best thing that happened at school today and one worst thing.
- I promise to complete all the experiences in *Champions in Life*.

Make a Declaration

Making a declaration announce something firmly, revealing who you are and what matters to you.

- I really like you!
- I give really great hugs!
- I am a *Champion in Life*!

Here are more examples of negative and positive communication that you might say inside your mind:

Negative Communication	Positive Communication
There's nothing I can do.	I will think about alternatives that might help.
That's just the way I am.	I can choose a different approach.
I wish I didn't have to do that.	I will choose an appropriate way to do that.
I can't.	I can!

When you want to communicate something, first listen to your ideas from your courageous "inner self." Ask yourself, "What do I want?"

Then, use your "outer self" to communicate your ideas, feelings, or needs to someone else, or a group of people.

Finally, ask yourself, "Did I get what I wanted?"

Yes! That's great! Keep going with what is next.
No! That's okay! Simply start again with, "What do I want?"

Communicate

Experience 1
Listen to Your "Inner Self" through Mindful Meditation

You will be challenged by this experience to communicate with, and listen to, your "inner self," the deepest part of you. This experience is what is known as mindful meditation, where you learn how to be your own best friend, your own mentor, your own guide.

This is actually such a fun, rewarding, and deeply satisfying meditation. Each time you visit this mindful place, recall all of the optimal mental health skills learned thus far, and note your growth in accessing your source of power, your "inner self."

You will be engaging in positive self-talk. You are communicating with your deepest levels of consciousness, the subconscious and intuition. Your "subconscious" is the part of your mind and brain that is not the focus of your current attention, but it is still there and operating. Your subconscious mind always says "yes" to what your conscious mind says. So, it is in your self-interest to ask or assert positive thoughts so that you gain agreement and support from your subconscious mind. Further, you may find yourself asking these types of questions as you go about your daily activities, as a form of mindful meditation.

You will be asking questions that open up the size of your listening and provide access to your "inner self." The size or space of your listening equals the size of the possibilities open to you.

Questions about advice, family, friends, relationships, activities, and goals are often good kinds of questions to ask when you want to open yourself up to deeper levels of knowing.

Some examples:

"What actions can I take to . . . ?"
"How can I better . . . ?"
"What is a good way of approaching . . . ?"
"What is my next step in . . . ?"

Questions to ask yourself should require more than a "yes" or "no" answer. This will give you an opportunity to communicate verbally with your "inner self." A "yes" or "no" answer does not give much of a chance for extended communication.

At this time, write down three questions of your own about anything you want to know about. Allow yourself plenty of time to reflect upon your questions. Take as much time as you require.

1.

2.

3.

Now, go deeper using mindful meditation.

You have the power to listen to your "inner self," at your deepest level. You can access this deepest inner place in the technique you are about to do. At this time, formally *choose* to go to this place by saying, "I choose to go to a deeper place within myself; I choose to know myself at a deeper level."

Please read the following three paragraphs slowly and deliberately. Read them several times, so you can recall the steps when your eyes are closed. You can also read them out loud, record them, and then play them back to complete the experience.

Next, breathe deeply for a few moments and relax your entire body, starting at your feet, then your legs, torso, and finally your head.

Then close your eyes for this mindful meditation:

Imagine yourself walking down a clear path through a beautiful forest area. It is a safe place to just let yourself go, to let your thoughts wander freely. You are alone and feel very safe and protected.

You see in front of you in the distance a small and beautiful house or other welcoming structure. You are drawn to this wonderful place by some powerful force, a very bright light that does not hurt your eyes to look at; in fact, it feels good to look at it. It draws you closer, and closer, and closer. You want to get closer and closer to the brilliant, bright light. The closer you get to the source of the light, the better you feel inside.

You are now only a few feet away from the source of the brilliant light, and you see a teacher or mentor whom you love and trust and who wishes you well . . . you are now only inches away from this guide, who asks you for your three questions. Listen with an open mind to whatever your guide communicates.

Open your eyes and write down the *answers* to your three questions now:

1.

2.

3.

Reflect upon the answers. The specifics of what you saw are not of great importance: your teacher may turn out to be someone you don't know, someone you do know, or even just an energy form or presence, and you may meet any place from a small cottage to a beautiful house of worship. Picture whatever works well for you. And, it may be different *each time* you do this mindful meditation. After doing this meditation, answer the following questions to yourself and then, if you would like, interact about them with one other person who is fully supportive of your inquiry:

1. Were the questions and answers ones that you would have expected?

2. Which answers were helpful?

3. What was the source of the light for you?

As you go about your daily life, be present to your experiences—or said another way, fully "experience your experiences"—as they are powerfully rich and beautiful and full of meaning and joy! And, most importantly, you are the source of your experiences, which come from deep inside of you.

Communicate

Experience 2
Make a Request

Everyone who is a *Champion in Life* needs others people to whom they can express their life purpose or request help for projects and for taking steps along the way to making their dreams a reality. You will need others in our life who are aligned with what you feel is important. You need good teammates!

Determine what you want to make happen and make a request to someone. What was your request?

Now write down what happened. Did they help you with your request? Yes! Hurray! That's a great connection!

No! That's no problem. It is simply interesting information. Think about what happened and who said what. What could you do differently the next time you communicate your request?

Space for Writing and Drawing

Communicate

Experience 3
Make a Promise

The instructions are simple, but this experience is full of feeling and accomplishment.

★

Make a promise.

Keep your promise.

Describe how it felt to make and keep your promise.

Space for Writing and Drawing

Communicate

How Did You Do?

Assess yourself on how you did on this skill. Ask yourself these questions:
- Did you complete all of the experiences for this skill?
- Describe which experience was the most meaningful to you.
- In the space below, draw 1 to 5 stars. Give yourself at least 1 star for completing all the experiences and up to 5 stars if you feel you did great on this skill overall.

Meet with Your Parent

Take a look back at everything you did for this skill and choose something to share with your parent. You can choose to share something you:
- learned about yourself
- are feeling
- created or made
- are doing to flourish and build your optimal mental health
- want to ask your parent about
- want to ask your parent to help you do
- and more

It is up to you to choose what you want to share about this skill. Remember, this is one meeting in your life when it is all about *you*, so you can practice having optimal mental health. There are no right or wrong answers! Your meeting doesn't have to be perfect. Give it a try!

Champions in Life

CERTIFICATE OF ACCOMPLISHMENT

Optimal Mental Health Superstar Award
for Completing Skill 8

Communicate

---

completed all of the experiences of the Communicate skill.

Let Your Star Shine!

Skill 9

Contribute

Contribute to other people in ways that express what matters to you.

Contribute

When you "contribute," you bring about a result, something that was not there prior to your contribution. It means to give to yourself and to others. There is always a before and after snapshot of the situation that you contributed to.

When you contribute, you make a difference. To contribute means to give your unique gifts to others.

What do you want to contribute? Your "inner self" qualities like hope and inspiration? Your "outer self" qualities like courage, leadership, and communication?

To what do you want to contribute? To a better world? Happier people? More love and less hate? More kindness and less meanness? Healthier people? Stronger friendships?

Recall your purpose statement. Recall your commitments. Your contributions are an expression of your purpose and commitments.

When you contribute, it is very similar to when you achieve. Just like with achievement, you are going for what your *dreams* tell you—not what your fears tell you. Are you going to contribute at the level of a *Champion in Life*? Prove it with your actions!

In the experiences for this skill, set your own intended results. Make a contribution that challenges you. Risk putting yourself out there and sharing who you are. Put more effort into this than anything you have done in the playbook so far. Think about what is important to you. Make contributions worthy of a *Champion in Life*!

The following three experiences will require a contribution to "Self," "Other," and "All." You will make a contribution to yourself, then to another person, and finally to the broader community or the world.

Contribute

Experience 1
Contribute to Your Self

"I want to contribute and give these gifts to myself in the following way:"

"The following outcomes will happen or exist to prove to myself that I made this contribution:"

"I felt the following emotions and feelings when I made this contribution to myself:"

Space for Writing and Drawing

Contribute

Experience 2
Contribute to Another Person

"I want to contribute and give these gifts to another person—such as my friend, someone in my family, or someone else I know—in the following ways:"

"The following outcomes will happen or exist to prove to myself that I made this contribution:"

"I felt the following emotions and feelings when I made this contribution to another person:"

Space for Writing and Drawing

Contribute

Experience 3
Contribute to a Group of People

"I want to contribute and give these gifts to a group of people—such as classmates, my community, or a cause that is important to me—in the following ways:"

"The following outcomes will happen or exist to prove to myself that I made this contribution:"

"I felt the following emotions and feelings when I made this contribution to a group of people:"

Space for Writing and Drawing

Contribute

How Did You Do?

Assess yourself on how you did on this skill. Ask yourself these questions:

- Did you complete all of the experiences for this skill?
- Describe which experience was the most meaningful to you.
- In the space below, draw 1 to 5 stars. Give yourself at least 1 star for completing all the experiences and up to 5 stars if you feel you did great on this skill overall.

Meet with Your Parent

Take a look back at everything you did for this skill and choose something to share with your parent. You can choose to share something you:

- learned about yourself
- are feeling
- created or made
- are doing to flourish and build your optimal mental health
- want to ask your parent about
- want to ask your parent to help you do
- and more

It is up to you to choose what you want to share about this skill. Remember, this is one meeting in your life when it is all about *you*, so you can practice having optimal mental health. There are no right or wrong answers! Your meeting doesn't have to be perfect. Give it a try!

Champions in Life

CERTIFICATE OF ACCOMPLISHMENT

Optimal Mental Health Superstar Award
for Completing Skill 9

Contribute

_____

completed all of the experiences of the Contribute skill.

Let Your Star Shine!

Skill 10

Celebrate You

Acknowledge accomplishments that are important to you,
and celebrate what inspires you for the future.

Celebrate You

The final skill is learning to celebrate you! Celebrate achievements that are important to you. It is a really fun skill, and at the same time, it is seriously important for optimal mental health.

You will be holding a celebration that is all about you. You will share what you want to say, about the results that you recognize as important, with people you want to invite. It is *your* celebration!

Your celebration can be as big or as small as you want it to be. This playbook has prepared you to hold your special celebration.

You could just invite your parent—the one who has been your connection throughout the playbook. But you could also expand the invitation list. You can invite your parent(s), siblings, friends, other family members, teachers you like, or anyone else you care about and trust. Be proud of what you have accomplished, and share the importance of optimal mental health and flourishing.

You optimize your mental health when you acknowledge and celebrate meeting your own wants and needs. It is a great skill to be able to acknowledge and celebrate your own self-driven accomplishments.

Some people get uncomfortable with celebrating the accomplishments of their "inner self." They have a negative conversation going on in their head that doesn't enable them to celebrate their own choices and wins. So don't let others' point of view dampen your spirit! Choose your invitees for their openness to building up mental health. And then they can have their own special celebration, too!

The "celebrate you" skill further helps you develop a sense of "self," and as stated earlier, self-awareness is the number one protective factor in ensuring optimal mental health.

Celebrate You

Experience 1
Optimal Mental Health

Do you recall the scale from the Introduction? Using the optimal mental health scale, where did you start and where are you now?

Consider what you have learned or experienced. Sometimes flourishing requires making a choice, even if life isn't perfect, to believe in yourself and know you are going for it. You are always growing with resilience in the direction of your hopes and dreams!

Put an "X" over the number that represents where you feel you were at the *beginning* of the playbook, and a circle around the number you feel you are at *now*.

Champions in Life
Optimal Mental Health Scale

-5   -4   -3   -2   -1   0   +1   +2   +3   +4   +5

← Low mental health   Optimal mental health and flourishing →

Space for Writing and Drawing

Celebrate You

Experience 2
Your Champions in Life Statement

You will be sharing a statement at your celebration.

This is your time to shine, so don't hold back. Put aside your concerns about being self-centered. It's not about that at all. You are celebrating one of the hardest things for people to celebrate. For some reason, people find it hard to celebrate their inner accomplishments and their optimal mental health. You will be showing people how to do it!

As you prepare your statement, remember the feeling behind this quote:

We ask ourselves, "Who am I to be brilliant, gorgeous, talented, and fabulous?"
Actually, who are you not to be?
—Marianne Williamson

Now prepare your statement by completing the following questions and writing everything out on the next pages. Celebrate your truly meaningful accomplishments, and feel proud. You deserve to feel great!

Champions in Life Statement to Read at Your Celebration

Thank you for coming to my celebration. Today, we are celebrating my completion of the *Champions in Life* playbook. I have optimized my mental health by learning 10 Essential Skills. And in the future, if you do this, I look forward to attending a celebration of you, too!

I have a statement I would like to share with you.

- I believe that a *Champion in Life* is someone who:

- I am a *Champion in Life* because I:

- The most meaningful skill I learned was:

- My favorite experience was when I:

- The area of my life where I made my biggest changes using the *Champions in Life* playbook are (for example, sharing emotions, school, relationship with my parents, relationship with my brother or sister, my ability to handle changes, how I feel about myself, my sense of hope and inspiration for the future):

- A *Champion in Life* is always thinking about what to accomplish next, where to improve and demonstrate that I am growing in the direction of my dreams. I want to continue to learn about:

- I never knew this about myself, but now I know I can:

Space for Writing and Drawing

Space for Writing and Drawing

Celebrate You

Experience 3
Your Celebration

It is time to hold your celebration! You can set it up by yourself, but also keep your parent informed. They may even want to help you set it up if you ask them.

- Choose a date and time that works for you and your parent or parents.

- Make a list of the people you want to attend. It is okay if you just want to celebrate with your parent, but you will gain more emotional connection if you invite other people too.

- Invite the people to attend by phone, text, email, asking them in person, or whatever works. You can use this invitation language, or write your own:

"Hi _____, I completed the *Champions in Life* playbook and learned 10 Essential Skills to optimize my mental health. It was challenging to learn new skills, but I did it all, so it is time to celebrate together! As the playbook says, 'You are either building up your mental health, or letting the world tear it down.' I have learned to talk about mental health as a positive thing. You don't just talk about mental health when there is something wrong—mental health is something to work on and celebrate every day. I am inviting you because you are an important person in my life, so I want to share with you what I experienced. You are invited to a celebration at [time] on [date] where I live. Only your 'presence' is requested. No 'presents' are needed! I will have light snacks and beverages. Just so you know, I may ask you to say something *you* feel about how I am growing. Other than that, just enjoy yourself. Oh, and I'll probably want to thank you for being in my life. Finally, I look forward to coming to a celebration of *you* whenever you want to have one. Thanks!"

- Hold the celebration in a location where people can relax and just be themselves. There's no need to spend lots of money on decorations. If that is something you enjoy and like to express, then by all means, decorate with streamers or drawings. But put most of your energy into your *Champions in Life* Statement. This is about *you* and your optimal mental health!

- When everyone is seated, ask for their attention.

- Reread out loud the invitation you sent. It serves as a reminder to everyone that this is different than other kinds of events.

- Read your *Champions in Life* Statement.

- If there is something you wrote, drew, filmed, made, or created that you especially liked, then share it with everyone at the celebration.

- Thank the special people, like your parent, who supported you as you completed the playbook.

- Then read the following paragraph to the people at the celebration:
"Now, it's your turn! Is there anything you would like to say? Have you noticed anything you want to share about how I have been growing on the inside? Do you want to say anything about the importance of mental health and well-being in your own life?"

- Finally, thank everyone for coming and for being in your life!

You did it! You celebrated optimal mental health and flourishing! You celebrated you!

Space for Writing and Drawing

Champions in Life

CERTIFICATE OF ACCOMPLISHMENT

Optimal Mental Health Superstar Award
for Completing Skill 10

Celebrate You

_____

completed all of the experiences of the Celebrate You skill.

Let Your Star Shine!

Your Champions in Life Award!

You've done it! You have completed all the experiences to learn all of the 10 Essential Skills!

You know that you are either building up your mental health every day, or letting the world tear it down.

As a *Champion in Life,* you will continue to grow in the direction of your dreams. Find other experiences to add to your playbook. Always put your optimal mental health first!

You are now conferred the title: *Champion in Life*!

Congratulations! Hurray!

Fill out your award on the next page with your name. If you involved your parent in the *Champions in Life* playbook, then ask them to sign their name at the bottom of the award, along with any words they want to write, such as, "I'm proud of you!" or "I love you!" or "Congratulations!"

The authors of *CHAMPIONS IN LIFE* do proclaim
upon your honorable word that

_____

(your name)

completed all of the
Champions in Life playbook skills
to the best of your abilities

and are hereby conferred the title

CHAMPION IN LIFE!

Postscript

The Power of This Work

Teens and parents, you may be wondering why this playbook and the 10 Essential Skills work to optimize your mental health. They work for two reasons:

1. *You* and your spirit want to soar! Teens are naturally drawn to dreams, purpose, hope, and inspiration—all of which are powerful mental health protective factors. And the playbook is self-guided, so you can experience optimal mental health at your own pace.

2. The authors spent decades extensively researching, conducting clinical work, and pursuing their commitment to the optimal mental health and well-being of teens and all people. Their research-based, evidence-based, high impact practices come from the fields of social-emotional learning, positive psychology, educational psychology, and human development. This playbook brings to you their Integrated Self Model™ and all of the powerful methods of their impactful, one-on-one *Champions* program for teens.

This postscript offers a brief summary of the work and research behind the *Champions in Life* playbook.

Optimizing Mental Health

The 10 Essential Skills in the *Champions in Life* playbook optimize teens' mental health. Teens aspire to a higher standard of excellence for a better life and a better world. They are requesting the opportunity to build a new value system, one based upon happiness, self-awareness, high self-esteem, and mental health and well-being.

Champions in Life guides teens in the general age range of 12 to 18 years to make a successful transition from childhood, through adolescence and puberty, to young adulthood. *Champions in Life* gives teens the support they need to envision their bright future by imparting mental health and well-being competencies, such as internal motivation, resilience, and a sense of purpose.

By completing the playbook, teens and their parents learn how to prioritize mental health and well-being. Teens can share more meaningful experiences with their parents and families.

The *Champions in Life* playbook helps teens define what a flourishing, healthy "self" feels like, as well as how to frame challenges and contribute to others. Teens want to gain competencies that are relevant to them and their future.

Teens want to:

- learn for themselves what optimal mental health, well-being, and flourishing look and feel like;
- understand their own emotions and what makes them happy;
- know how to assess and impact all the dimensions of their own health—mind, body, and soul; and
- maintain high levels of well-being in school and life.

The *Champions in Life* playbook empowers what is possible for teens versus focusing upon problems to fix. Every young person is on a unique path of personal discovery to create their own destiny. They want to live a life of total health, wholeness, and accomplishment—to the level of their dreams.

Teens can learn to create their own model of "self," to dramatically impact the quality of their life. With the *Champions in Life* playbook, they can take away a system of learning that empowers the understanding and expression of their own unique potential. The skills learned through the playbook will stay with them throughout their lives.

The playbook does not talk down to teens, but rather challenges them with new concepts that they learn experientially and can return to time and again to experience new levels of happiness, health, and well-being.

Teens want to change and grow! This is fundamental to who they are. A natural life force resides deep within teens. Some call this undeniable force the drive to manifest their destiny.

Changes can happen cognitively, emotionally, physically, or all of these holistically—mind, body, soul. It is in a teen's self-interest to change—they benefit! If a teen is constantly changing anyway, they may as well take charge of the processes of change and go in the direction they want.

By placing the teen reader as the leading character, the playbook becomes customized to each teen's unique personality, character, talents, passions, issues, and concerns. The teen reader can choose to focus on areas of special interest, such as passions, academics, personal growth, relationships, self-esteem, and more.

Teens who have experienced the work of *Champions in Life* report that they are more at ease, less anxious, feel a new sense of self-responsibility, and express themselves more freely with family and friends and in school. They learn to produce results in their day-to-day lives that align with their own sense of purpose and vision. They learn to become the author of their own life story, the architect of their life structures, the artist of their life's painting.

Studies find that 75% of success in life is due to non-cognitive factors such as motivation, self-awareness, emotional intelligence, and passion for pursuing an area of interest. Schools are not doing enough to impart these competencies.

Teens and their families want more—they want real-life tools that proactively teach them how to envision and pursue a happy, healthy, and flourishing life. Parents everywhere and of all backgrounds have the highest hopes for these remarkable possibilities for their teens.

Believing in possibilities takes a shift in thinking and considerable courage. Possibilities are potential states of being that take you beyond your current thinking to new perspectives heretofore unavailable to you. Specifically, new psychological or cognitive possibilities are always available to you, new pathways to create a new you and new life.

This is often exciting and transforms your mindset from resignation to a sense of possibilities, along with concomitant positive emotions and new life circumstances; it is like seeing current circumstances through a new lens.

Teen Mental Health Crisis

Parents are demanding more emotional supports for their teens, and teens are demanding more skills to be able to experience the life of their dreams.

Teens currently do not have a framework and mental model of understanding their own mental health and well-being to be able to express what is going on inside. Parents and caregivers can ensure their teens are equipped with the latest best practices for prevention, and not wait until treatment is necessary.

According to a recent study by the national Center for Disease Control's National Center for Health Statistics, parents *think* they are offering emotional support during the critical teen years, but teens *disagree*. Therefore, teens are suffering in silence with nowhere to turn.

External pressures—without the internal constitution to meet the excessive demands of modern life—can lead to "disintegration," or the process of losing one's sense of "self." A "disintegrated self" is a false "self" learned through contemporary culture, with its limited acceptable values, customs, behaviors, and emotions. These forces are extremely powerful, omnipresent, ubiquitous, and destructive. These forces can be destructive to the full expression of a person's own sense of "self" and of their own inner sense of a destiny in life. They can even be destructive to basic human instincts and emotions that serve as a source of inner motivation to grow, change, and make a unique contribution to the greater good.

Psychologist Dr. Carol Gilligan developed research on girls' development while at Harvard University at a time when most prior research had been done on boys. She found that girls age 12 and 13 know exactly what they want to be when they grow up. However, starting at age 14, girls start to doubt their own voice and begin to grow more silent. Now, the authors of *Champions in Life* have found that *all* teens are on this precipice.

The dominance of screen time in everyone's life has contributed to more "dissociation," a clinical term meaning that people are numb and separated from their emotions and experiences. Further, the online world can be a manipulative environment that presses teens to take on behaviors and thoughts that others dictate.

Additionally, with 24-7 access to worldwide news—covering wars, climate disasters, depleted natural resources, and other overwhelming tensions—existential anxiety and depression can cover teens' day-to-day experiences like a heavy, wet blanket, keeping teens from fully experiencing the joy, happiness, and love that are available through their relationships and daily experiences.

While schools sometimes provide *some* minor socio-emotional supports, these are taught in the service of advancing academics, propping teens up to just keep going, rather than in service of prioritizing a lifetime of optimal mental health. Schools are *not* teaching how to optimize mental health and flourish. In fact, the overwhelming approach in most schools is to test and grade to fit pre-determined measures that make teens feel like data points, rather than generative, creative, and valuable human beings.

Teens have learned that everything else is more important—and more worthy of time and attention—than their own mental health and well-being. Discussions about grades, careers, and material goods far outpace discussions about internal values, commitment, and self-awareness. Certainly "survival" is important. But teens' birthright is to "flourish," and not just "survive."

Optimal mental health is *not* just the absence of mental illness. It is the ability to flourish. Everyone who cares about teens can agree that happy, healthy, and flourishing teens do not do harm to themselves or others.

But a flourishing life doesn't just happen. Parents and caregivers need to join with educators, counselors, and medical practitioners to proactively teach teens the 10 Essential Skills to optimize mental health. They can all come together to protect teens from the stressors of modern life and help teens realize their bright future.

The Integrated Self Model™ informed the 10 Essential Skills. The entire model can be integrated into family culture, medical pediatric assessments, school counseling, school curriculum, and community programs to reduce and prevent mental illness and empower mental health and well-being. The model can teach self-agency, resilience, hope, purpose, an ability to experience both positive and negative emotions, and many more attributes.

Reintegrating the Self

Teens need to make a choice. They can simply survive, and get by in life, or they can flourish in their own way—based upon the dreams they have for their life.

Teens have not been taught what a "self" is, with all the complexities and refined distinctions of "inner self" versus "outer self," nor how to use them to create a happy, healthy, flourishing life. Much of teen life is externally guided, where they do not know another model. They have some of the components, but these are not yet complete nor integrated.

An analogy would be a child's kaleidoscope; when first viewed all that can be seen are numerous colors in blurry patterns. After learning how to make adjustments, first to the left, then to the right, and with numerous iterations, the viewer sees a clearer picture, filled with beautiful and distinct colors.

To learn about the "self," it becomes more and more important for teens to share the deep feelings they have about themselves, their life, and the world condition.

Sometimes emotional distress, such as feelings of anxiety or depression, can happen naturally as part of personal development and if explored, can propel a teen forward. These symptoms do *not* mean there is anything "wrong" with the teen. Rather, they suggest a process of growth and evolution into their ideal "self."

Teens' state of "disintegration" requires what Polish psychologist Kazimierz Dabrowski identified as "reintegration." This involves a new level of deeper understanding, self-awareness, and self-acceptance. This path to reintegration involves the teen reconciling themselves to existential questions and distress and learning to manage these feelings through choices that add meaning to their life. This playbook teaches this process of reintegration.

If teens want a future in which they thrive, and not merely survive, then they will need to shift their mindset and make choices that shape their own current and future realities. This process is less about removing teens from ongoing difficulties, but rather providing *practice* in acquiring the tools to handle them, and relieving teens from having the difficulties take over their life.

The playbook espouses the psychology of well-being and the integrated connection between mind, body, and soul. Optimal mental health is when all parts of the "self" are integrated, working together, in sync, and in balance.

The Integrated Self Model™

The authors developed the Integrated Self Model™, which is a framework to understand the "self" and the whole person through cognitive and positive psychology attributes that teens can learn experientially. Parents, educators, and health professionals can teach these attributes to teens to strengthen their well-being.

The "self" is important to know and understand, because it mediates the *inner* life with the *outer* life to determine realities and shape a positive life course.

The Integrated Self Model™ (Brzycki and Brzycki, 2009, 2016, 2019) incorporates concepts from:

- educational psychology—the science of how people learn and grow;
- developmental psychology—the study of the "self" as the sum of dynamic component parts; and
- positive psychology—the study of ways people can flourish in their lives.

The Integrated Self Model™ (also known as the iSelf Model™) provides a holistic and multidimensional understanding of 40 attributes, which are the integrated parts that make up a "self." Attributes from the Integrated Self Model™ are mentioned throughout the playbook.

The self attributes are shaped by and, in turn, shape external and cultural experiences.

Teaching teens about even just one of the attributes serves to strengthen all of the other attributes. The process works like a mobile, a work of art that has many interconnected parts moving freely in the air.

Each part of the mobile is like one of the attributes. When you move one part of the mobile—with either the touch of a hand or a breath of air—all the other parts of the mobile move and get repositioned. If a teen develops the attribute of self-efficacy, in the same manner as with the mobile, they will develop other attributes, such as self-esteem. When one attribute changes, as in a mobile, all attributes are impacted to varying degrees.

Interacting with the attributes heightens self-awareness exponentially, which helps teens grow and expand their ability to see and achieve their potential. When explored, the self attributes become enlightening and inspiring. They come together for the teen to create a whole "self." They open up a world of possibilities for a purposeful, fulfilling, and happy life.

Here is the diagram of the Integrated Self Model™:

The Integrated Self Model™

Mind – Body – Soul

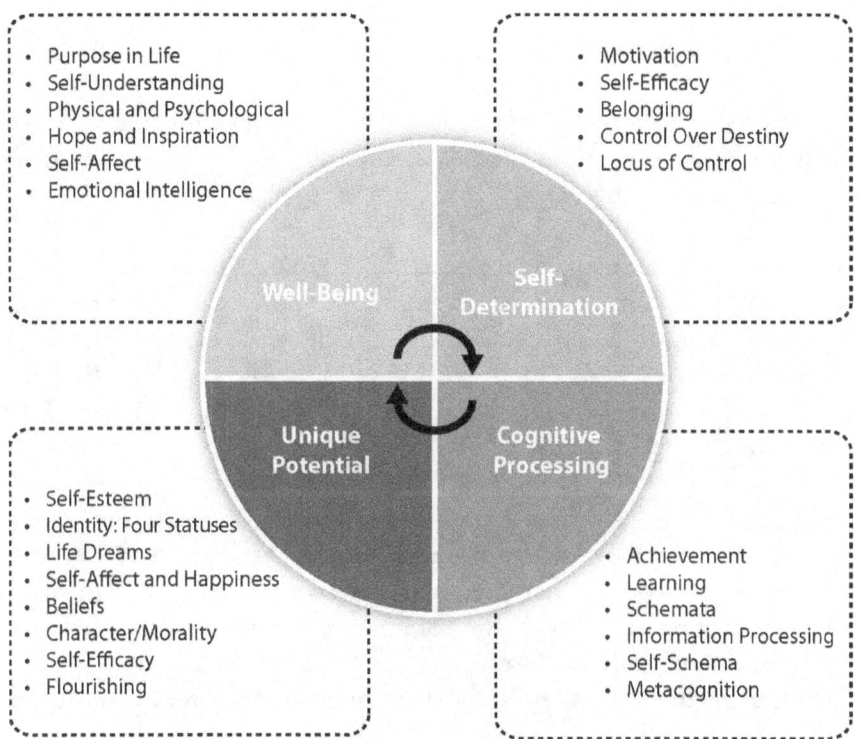

- Purpose in Life
- Self-Understanding
- Physical and Psychological
- Hope and Inspiration
- Self-Affect
- Emotional Intelligence

- Motivation
- Self-Efficacy
- Belonging
- Control Over Destiny
- Locus of Control

- Self-Esteem
- Identity: Four Statuses
- Life Dreams
- Self-Affect and Happiness
- Beliefs
- Character/Morality
- Self-Efficacy
- Flourishing

- Achievement
- Learning
- Schemata
- Information Processing
- Self-Schema
- Metacognition

Well-Being

Self-Determination

Unique Potential

Cognitive Processing

External and Cultural Experiences

About the Authors

Elaine J. Brzycki, Ed.M., and Henry G. Brzycki, Ph.D., are renowned positive psychologists who have generated a body of research-based, evidence-based work to impact the human condition and make the world a better place. Exploring their life purpose for 40 years, they have helped people create happy, healthy, and flourishing lives.

As the leading experts in teen mental health and well-being, they invented the Integrated Self Model™, which is transforming education and counseling worldwide—used by pediatricians, psychologists, teachers, and parents.

They have authored five bestselling books, numerous articles, and personal and professional development workshops. Utilized in over 50 countries, their work has led to a new worldwide consciousness about the importance of self-understanding and placing mental health and well-being at the center of a good and thriving life. Their organizations, The Brzycki Group and The Center for the Self in Schools, have pioneered and created the field of mental health prevention techniques.

This self-help book for teens offers breakthrough methods from the Brzyckis' proven *Champions* program, developed by Henry, during his doctoral studies at The Pennsylvania State University, and by Elaine, during her graduate work at the Harvard University Graduate School of Education. She studied with the foremost women's developmental psychologist, Dr. Carol Gilligan, among others. Elaine was inspired by Harvard's Project on Human Potential, which transformed the world's understanding of the potential of humankind.

Share Your Experiences with the Authors

If you want to share examples of how the *Champions in Life* skills have worked for you, the authors would be interested in hearing from you. Feel free to share your experiences with them at:

brzyckigroup.com

Though the authors may not be able to respond to every teen who reaches out, they will happily celebrate all of your good work on yourself!

Post to the Instagram Account

Please feel free to make full use of the Instagram account set up for teens who are becoming *Champions in Life*. You can post your ideas, accomplishments, full self-expression, times when you flourished, and more.

champions_in_life_teen

www.ingramcontent.com/pod-product-compliance
Lightning Source LLC
Chambersburg PA
CBHW081532120626
46550CB00009B/2701